The Scourge of Demons

The Scourge of Demons

A Classic Manual (1576) on Exorcism and Spiritual Warfare

by
Fr. Girolamo Menghi, OFM

Translated by
Fr. Robert Nixon, OSB

2025
Slaying Dragons Press Classics

www.SlayingDragonsPress.com
2025

IMPRIMATUR FROM THE 1623 VENICE EDITION

1623, the 4th day of September

Imprimatur

Fr. Francisco Carenus
PROFESSOR OF THEOLOGY
VICAR OF THE MOST HOLY INQUISITION, MILAN

Fr. Aloysius Bariola
CONSULTOR TO THE HOLY OFFICE
FOR THE MOST ILLUSTRIOUS LORD CARDINAL ARCHBISHOP
[OF VENICE]

Reviewed and Approved
FOR THE MOST EXCELLENT SENATE
[OF VENICE]

TABLE OF CONTENTS

FOREWORD

W HILE TAKING a course at the *Teresianum* in Rome on Ignatian discernment of spirits a couple of decades ago, I recall the discomfiture of many of the gentler students (priests, religious, seminarians, and some laity) as the professor discussed Ignatius' treatment of spiritual influences on the soul and their various sources. The repeated naming of evil spirits as one of the causes seemed to engender a sense of unease; a mix of the disappointment children experience when they learn that the Easter bunny isn't real and the existential apoplexy one feels upon learning that someday one will have to answer to God for his every thought, word, action and omission – along with the perfect restitution that will be demanded in the order of perfect justice.

Such a person most likely isn't reading this now.

If it is a cause of wonder that those consecrated to the service of God in the Church would reel at the notion of ordinary demonic influences that touch us all, it ought not surprise us that there are bishops, priests, and religious who would rather leave souls to languish under extraordinary demonic influences than sully their hands with this ministry.

Why is this? I can only assume it has something to do with a lack of either faith, hope, or charity.

- Some do not believe in the Deposit of Faith that includes in its articles the existence of multitudes of demons.
- Others are afraid of what the devil will do if they engage in this ministry, exhibiting more fear of Satan than of the Lord.
- Still others simply couldn't be bothered to take seriously those who complain of their demonic suffering, sometimes in ways that are not the most articulate, but suffer they most certainly do.

Of those faults against the theological virtues just mentioned, the most common seems to be the second one; that against hope. I question whether those same effete and timorous souls tremble at the thought of entering a church with the Blessed Sacrament exposed; whether they exhibit a similar amount of fear of the Lord in each Mass they attend or celebrate. It's almost surreal to think of a priest who doesn't hesitate to hold the Almighty in his fingertips yet is frightened of a little spiritual cockroach that very One has created.

This book was written for those who share the Catholic Faith in its entirety, for those whose hope in Christ is born of His love for us and one's trust in Him, for, as St. John says, *true love casts out all fear* (1 Jn 4:18). The sagacious counsels herein contained are the fruit of a centuries-long distillation process, a sort of extrapolation of the 21 numbers provided for exorcists in Chapter 1 of *Titulus XII* of the *Roman Ritual.*

Worthy of mention here is Menghi's perspicacious understanding of human nature and the pitfalls that await the unvigilant soul. He counsels the exorcist to not seek celebrity, since self-aggrandizement is an obstacle to the glory of God. Yet although this is also clearly stated in the *Roman Ritual*'s counsels for exorcists, the point is valid for all priests. Priesthood and celebrity are a bad cocktail, and rarely does it improve a priest's spiritual life to expose himself to the masses save those few cases in which God has given the priest, as was the case with Fulton Sheen, a grace to remain humble despite the attention and adulation. The mix of our fallen nature and the baggage that comes with notoriety can put the treasure of one's vocation in a precarious position. It's simply not worth the risk to presume one has such a grace.

Despite all the sound doctrine and discipline and pastoral teaching Menghi provides us, I would disagree with him on one point. For all the reasons he offers in favor of public and private exorcisms as legitimate exercise of this ministry, public exorcisms should be avoided at all costs for the following reasons:

- Anonymity of the afflicted – their dignity must be preserved.
- Protection of the priest from vainglory (celebrity and priesthood are never a good mix).
- Propriety – discretion is the order of the day, and some things ought not be offered as a public spectacle.
- Spiritual situation of would-be gawkers – who can guarantee that those witnessing such an event are in a state of grace?

- Morbid curiosity is a vice and ought not be fomented.
- Possibility of the presence of Satanists – they would like nothing more than to attend an exorcism and execute their rituals summoning more demons to militate against the exorcism.

Menghi clears up an important point. He states that innocent and righteous souls can also be afflicted – although many attribute some culpability to the afflicted when that is clearly not always the case. Nonetheless, in cases where one's own actions brought about this deplorable situation, the soul is worthy of the Church's tireless effort to seek first – not its liberation from demons – but the deliverance of the soul from sin and the surrender of the soul to the Heart of Christ in the bosom of the Church, the Sacrament of Salvation. Salvation, sanctification, and reparation are at the center of the Church's mission. If alleviation of suffering comes along with those goods, that is counted as a blessing and a further revelation of God's Mercy.

On the other hand, it must be remembered that at the center of this ministry is not the demon, nor the exorcist, nor even the afflicted member of Christ's Mystical Body. At the center of it all is Jesus Christ. Once this is well established and ingrained in the hearts and minds of both exorcist and energumen[1], the entire process, long and grueling as it may be, will work towards the glorification of God and the sanctification of both priest and victim who are united in offering a sacrifice worthy of our Lord and pleasing in His eyes. In this case, the liberation will take place at the exact time of our Lord's choosing. Not a second before or after. In all of this, the demon is forced to cooperate. As a result, the ministry of exorcism is indeed a *scourge of demons.*

---

[1] The name for one who is possessed.

Translator's Introduction

THE WORK which is presented in this volume is the famous *Flagellum Daemonum* ('The Scourge of Demons'), with the most significant and useful part in English translation for the first time.[1] This remarkable and historically important text was one of the very first published manuals on exorcism (appearing in print in 1576), and the first one to gain a wide and general circulation and acceptance. The author is Fr. Girolamo Menghi (1529–1609), a learned and devout Italian Franciscan friar, priest and theologian, with particularly extensive experience as an exorcist. Indeed, his reputation and authority on the practice of exorcism was such that he gained the appellation 'The Father of the Exorcist's Art.' His *Flagellum Daemonum* enjoyed vast popularity both in its own time and in the three centuries which followed,

---

[1] A partial translation (containing only the texts of the exorcisms themselves) was published by Gaetano Paxia in 2002.

1

appearing in well over twenty editions. During this time, it served as the definitive textbook and manual for priests involved in the conduct of exorcisms.

The work is written in a relatively accessible style and is intended to be readily comprehensible by the average parish priest, and is firmly grounded in scholastic theology. The list of authorities cited by Menghi is impressive indeed, and reflects the thoroughness of his research and the scope of his erudition. To these authorities, he adds his own extensive personal experience. Although intended as a guide for priests engaged in exorcism, the *Flagellum Daemonum* was also widely read by the laity and was popular even in nations which had fallen prey to the Protestant heresy.[2] The value and interest of the book for laypersons lies primarily in the insights it offers into the causes, conditions and typical symptoms of demonic possession and attacks by evil spirits and witchcraft.

Of course, exorcism had been practiced since the times of the early Church and throughout the Middle Ages. However, the 16th century saw a particular increase in the need for that ministry, with the outbreak of new waves of witchcraft across Europe which, at times, reached almost plague proportions. Such practices involved the invocation of malign spirits and demons, which were all-too-ready to vex and even take possession of many unfortunate susceptible individuals. In addition to the proliferation of the practice of the black arts in the 16th century, there was also another no less harmful and nefarious virus then infecting European Christendom—the heresies of Lutheranism, Calvinism, and other schismatic groups. In this context, Menghi's *Flagellum*, which was published with full ecclesiastical and civil approval, fulfilled an important and much needed role, providing detailed and balanced

---

[2] It seems that in many cases, persons who otherwise professed the errors of Protestantism had more faith in Catholic authors and rites in dealing with such serious matters.

instructions for exorcists, as well as particular prayers, rites, and formulae of exorcism.

The work consists of two principal parts. The first lays down general instructional guidelines for preparation, cautions, and discussions of what is permissible, appropriate, and helpful in liberating persons or places from demonic influences. The second part presents the actual texts and rubrics for some seven exorcisms.

This present volume includes the instructional guidelines in their entirety, augmented with certain chapters from another important work of Menghi, *Fustis Daemonum* (*The Cudgel of Demons*). Only the first two of the actual rites of exorcism are included in the volume. These provide a representative sample, especially the first one, which is the most detailed and comprehensive of the series. It should be emphasized that these exorcism prayers should not be used by any persons (whether laypersons or priests) without proper authorization from ecclesiastical authorities, and they are published for their historical and catechetical interest only.

Some observations should be made regarding translational choices. All Latin words are given in English, whereas Greek and Hebrew words (which are mainly sacred names or titles) have been retained in the original, with translations occasionally added as footnotes. Menghi, in common with most authors of the period, was somewhat inconsistent in his orthography of transliterated Hebrew words. In most cases, his spelling has been retained, except where the word in question is well-known in a now standardized spelling (such as *Adonai*).

Extremely long Latin sentences have sometimes been divided for the sake of readability. The commonly occurring word *conjuratio* (and its related forms) has generally been given as 'adjuration' or 'command,' since the English word 'conjure' has come to denote something quite different from its original meaning of 'solemnly command.' The word *obsessus* (and its related forms) has been translated either as 'possessed,' 'vexed,' or 'besieged,' depending upon the context. Clearly, the word 'obsessed' (though etymologically derived from '*obsessus*') has taken on a very different meaning in contemporary usage. It should be noted that the word 'possessed,' as it is used here, does not generally mean that the demon has taken full or complete control over the individual, but rather that it is dwelling within them in a vexatious manner.

Identification of verses of Sacred Scripture are provided only when they are potentially useful to the reader. As the formulae of exorcism are filled with Scriptural references, these have not all been identified. Readers familiar with the offices and liturgies of the Church, will, of course, recognize these without difficulty, just as Menghi's original readers would have. Where Menghi himself provides a scriptural reference in the text (which he does frequently), he does so by giving the book and chapter number alone, but not the verse, as was the practice of the time. This system of identification is perfectly adequate, and additional footnotes have not been added in such cases.

It is the hope of the translator that this work will be of interest not only to priests involved in the conduct of exorcism and to serious scholars of Catholic history, but also to Catholics everywhere. Among the contemporary literature, there is, unfortunately, a notable lacuna of serious writings in this field. On the one hand, there are works which tend to reduce demonic influences to merely psychological conditions; and, on the other hand, there are many works of a sensationalist nature, which reflect the influence of popular legends and cinematic dramatizations as much as the experiences of serious practitioners and authentic Church teachings.

This new translation of a classic text by the 'Father of the Exorcist's Art' will hopefully contribute to filling this lacuna. The importance and value of this can hardly be overstated, for the counsel to "know thine enemy" is never more critical than when that enemy is the Lord of Darkness and the Father of Lies himself.

Fr. Robert Nixon, OSB
Abbey of the Most Holy Trinity
New Norcia, Western Australia

List of Authorities Used by the Author in this Work

Pope St. Alexander I
Alexander de Ales[1]
Alphonsus Castrensis
St. Ambrose, Doctor of the Church
St. Augustine, Doctor of the Church
Bartolomeo Sibilla[2]
St. Bede the Venerable, Doctor of the Church
St. Bernard of Clairvaux, Doctor of the Church
Bernardine de Bustis
Boethius Severinus
St. Bonaventure, Doctor of the Church
Various Councils of the Church
Blessed Dionysius the Carthusian
St. Fulgentius, Doctor of the Church
The *Glossa Ordinaria*[3]

---

[1] A Franciscan theologian of the 12th and 13th centuries, who taught St. Bonaventure.
[2] A Dominican theologian of the 15th century.

Pope St. Gregory the Great, Doctor of the Church
Haymo, Bishop of Halberstadt
Henricus Arphius
St. Jerome, Doctor of the Church
St. Hilary [of Poitiers], Doctor of the Church
Hugh of St. Victor
Bl. Joachim di Fiore, Abbot
St. John Chrysostom
Bl. John Cassian, Abbot
St. John Damascene
Jean Gerson
Bl. John Duns Scotus
[Flavius] Josephus, [the author of] *The Jewish War*
St. Isidore of Seville, Doctor of the Church
Pope St. Leo the Great, Doctor of the Church
Louis de Blois
The Master of the Sentences [Peter Lombard]
The Master of the Histories [Peter Comestor]
The *Malleus Maleficarum*[4]
Michael Psellus
Nicholas de Lira
Paolo Grillandi[5]
Pietro Colonna Galatino[6]
Richard of Middleton
Rupert, Abbot [of Deutz]
Sylvester [Mazzolini] Prierias[7]
St. Thomas Aquinas, Doctor of the Church

---

[3] The *Glossa Ordinaria* was the standard and authoritative commentary on Scripture in the scholastic period.
[4] 'The Hammer of Witchcraft,' an authoritative text written by Heinrich Kramer, OP, and used as a manual by the Inquisition.
[5] A judge of the papal court, who presided over witch trials in the early 16th century.
[6] A Franciscan philosopher, theologian, and scholar of oriental languages (1460–1540).
[7] A Dominican theologian of 15th and 16th centuries, who was one of the most vigorous opponents of Luther.

CHAPTER I

THE FIRMNESS OF FAITH, PURITY OF CONSCIENCE AND
HUMILITY WHICH THE EXORCIST OUGHT TO HAVE BEFORE
HE BEGINS TO DEAL WITH DEMONS

WHOEVER DESIRES to trample over the serpents of hell rightly, easily, and without peril to his own salvation and that of others, ought to beware of all vain, unlawful, and superstitious practices. Among all the works of mercy, the task of commanding demons who have taken possession of human bodies is certainly the most laborious. But it is an operation which, if done through charity, without sin, and with the help of God, will merit eternal glory for those who undertake it.

Before all else, whoever would perform exorcisms must have indubitable trust in the mysteries of Jesus Christ and firm belief in the Catholic Faith. For performance of all miracles is to be ascribed to faith, and the office of exorcism is indeed such a miracle.

To this should be added purity of conscience, which is to be attained by true contrition of heart and honest and sincere sacramental confession. For even though a priest, by virtue of the power of ordination, prays in the person of the Church, nevertheless his prayer will be more efficacious when he beseeches God as one who is deserving to be heard. Sins which have been forgiven by God through true penitence are concealed from the devil. As experience has shown, the devil is incapable of raising accusations of such sins before the priest, especially if he commands him to silence through the power of God.

But where there has not been proper contrition and forgiveness of sins, demons (who perceive the hidden thoughts and movements of the human heart) will often raise such sins before the priest who attempts to exorcise them, thereby creating confusion and shame. Indeed, demons will often make not only true accusations of sins which are weighing on the priest's conscience, but will also often mix false accusations among the true ones.

But if this should happen, the exorcist should by no means desist from his work, for God does not grant to demons the authority to convict persons of sins—although He does permit them to make accusations, and even false ones at times. The exorcist ought to have the most profound humility as he undertakes his task, considering himself always to be a mere instrument of God, and knowing that he is able to achieve nothing at all except through the power and help of God.

An exorcist should never seek the praise or adulation of human beings for his work, but should take his joy only in the honor of almighty God and in the salvation of human souls. For if he does otherwise, he will not only forfeit all claim to genuine merit, but may even incur the guilt of sin.

Furthermore, a priest who cultivates true humility will be more effective as an exorcist. For demons are not able to tolerate the fragrance of genuine humility; and God gives

His gifts and graces more freely and generously to those who use them well and properly, for His own glory.

If the exorcist is well armed and prepared with these counsels and considerations, he may wage conflict with the devil with security and confidence, knowing that he is performing a work pleasing to and approved of by God, for he shall see that by his undertaking he is rendering blessing and glory to God.

CHAPTER II

THE PURITY OF CONSCIENCE WHICH THE PERSON POSSESSED
OUGHT TO CULTIVATE, AND HOW THE EXORCIST OUGHT TO
DETERMINE WITH CERTAINTY WHETHER OR NOT THE
PERSON IS REALLY POSSESSED

THE EXORCIST ought to urge and exhort the person possessed or vexed by a demon that they work on cleansing and purifying their conscience with the greatest diligence. This is firstly because their prayers and cries to God will then be more readily heard; secondly, it is because those whose consciences are polluted with unrepented and unconfessed sins and guilt are much more easily and frequently attacked by demons.

The exorcist should instruct the person who is subject to demonic afflictions to subject themselves to God with all humility, and to pray that (if it be in accordance with God's will) they will be liberated from whatever malign spirits are troubling or controlling them.

Next, the exorcist should undertake to determine whether or not the subject is really possessed or vexed by a demon. In doing this, he will ensure that the sacerdotal dignity and the serious work of exorcism is not treated lightly, nor vainly used without proper and serious justification.

The priest may know for certain that a demon is present when the person possessed is witnessed to say or to know something which, in their own capacity, they would not be able to say or to know. This could include, for example, details of things which have taken place in some distant location, or objects or happenings which are otherwise hidden from the person in question.

The priest may determine with probability (but not certainty) that a demonic entity is present if he witnesses the hands of the subject tremble when sacred words are said, or when they make sudden or unusual movements or spasms, or show pain and repulsion, at the mention of the sacraments, especially confession and the Eucharist, as well as the names of saints, and also when various divine prayers are said.

From the beginning, the exorcist should endeavor to compel the demon to reveal its presence. One method of doing this is to bind something sacred to the person (such as a relic of a saint, or a piece of paper with a line from Sacred Scripture written upon it). This should be done in such a way that the person is not aware of it.[1] If they display some unusual reaction to the presence of such a sacred object, it is a reliable indication of a diabolical presence.

But note well (contrary to what is said by detractors of this art), that demons who possess human bodies very rarely speak in Latin. The first cause of this is that the demons do not wish their presence to be known. A second reason is that demons use the physical faculties of the one whom they are possessing as an instrument. Therefore, a

---

[1] Translator's note: This may indicate either that the person is not aware that something is bound to them at all, or it may indicate that they are not aware of *what* is being bound to them.

demon who has taken possession of a person who speaks only their vernacular will not easily answer in Latin. Nor, for that matter, will a demon which has taken possession of an Italian person readily speak in French. For the tongue of the person possessed is accustomed and conditioned to a particular mode of speaking, and so will still speak more readily and more easily in their own accustomed language even when they are possessed by an evil spirit.[2]

---

[2] This does not imply that the demon is incapable of understanding Latin (or other languages), but rather that the vocal apparatus of the person possessed will be more fluent and comfortable with their own usual language.

CHAPTER III

WHETHER OBJECTS OF THE SENSES ARE ABLE TO EFFECT
DEMONS, AND THE BEST MANNER OF EMPLOYING SUCH
DEVICES

A N EXORCIST is indeed able to use objects of the senses against demons possessing or besieging a human body. Such objects of the senses include holy water, incense, sulfur, herbs, medicines, and a variety of other potions and substances. These all ought to be blessed and exorcized before being put to such a use.

There are many who object to the use of such devices, for a variety of reasons. Some reply will be offered to these objections. According to Richard of Middleton, even though herbs, musical sounds, and physical substances are not able, by their natural powers, to completely overcome demonic vexations (when they are permitted to happen by God), they are able to mitigate and alleviate such vexations considerably. And they may minimize the affliction to the point that it is virtually cured. They achieve this not by working on the demons themselves, since demons are spiritual beings and not liable to influence by any material thing, according to its purely natural properties. Rather, objects of the senses are able to have a beneficial effect on the person who is suffering.

All spiritual forces are able to produce more effect in a person who is pre-disposed to their influence. According to Aristotle, the act of the one acting has an effect only on a subject disposed to be responsive to that act. Therefore, the devil, who is the one acting, is only able to afflict a human being who has a disposition which is liable to such an affliction. But he will not be able to afflict a person whose disposition is entirely contrary to what he intends.

Consider, for example, the case of melancholy. A demon will readily be able to afflict with melancholy a person who is already temperamentally pre-disposed to that condition. But a person whose disposition and temperament are contrary to any feelings of melancholy will not be able to be affected by a demon to the same extent, and possibly not at all.

It is indisputable that objects of the senses, such as herbs, musical sounds, and many other things, are able to affect the disposition of the human body and therefore also the movement of the senses and feelings of the individual. A good example of this is herbs—some of these, when consumed, cause feelings of joy and energy, whereas others cause feelings of sorrow or lethargy. I say the same of music of different types, and Aristotle has demonstrated that diverse genres of music are able to give rise to different types of emotions in human beings. Boethius states the same thing, noting the usefulness of music in alleviating certain types of infirmities.

And, by means of objects of the senses which can affect a person's disposition, the devil becomes unable to vex them, or only to a very minor extent. If a person's natural disposition is very much to the contrary of that with which the demon is trying to afflict them, then the demon's power will be completely without effect.

Now, as we have noted earlier, certain herbs, musical sounds, and other objects of the senses are able to affect the disposition of the human body. By this means, they can annul the effects of demonic vexation. For example, if a demon afflicts a certain person with a debilitating sadness, and then certain herbs are given to the person which have the contrary effect, the vexatious sadness caused by the demon may be completely cancelled.

I am not saying, however, that the use of particular herbs, musical sounds, or other objects of the senses are able to affect a human being's disposition so strongly that they will then become completely immune to the vexations of demons. This is especially so in cases of persons suffering very severely from demonic possession or vexation.

It should be noted also that there are certain persons who argue that objects of the senses are able only to combat evil effects produced by other objects of the senses—such as herbs, or the unpropitious movements of the stars, etc. To refute this view, we cite Sacred Scripture. In 1 Samuel 16, it is stated that when Saul was vexed by an evil spirit, then David was able to alleviate his suffering by playing his lyre.[1] And in Tobit 6, the angel Raphael expels a demon from Sarah and Tobias by means of the intestines of a fish, saying that if he placed the liver of this fish over burning coals the smoke would expel all kinds of demons both from a man and a woman.[2] But this was done with the help of prayer and after maintaining sexual continence for three days, with the angel binding the demon after it was expelled.

What more shall I say? Pope St. Alexander I, in his first letter, instructs all priests to bless holy water for the people, following his own example. "We bless water

---

[1] See 1 Samuel 16: 14-23.
[2] See Tobit 6: 1-7 and 8:1-3.

containing salt," he writes, "so that all sprinkled with it may be sanctified and purified. We direct all priests to follow this practice. For if, by the adding of salt to water, Elisha the prophet was able to cure the sterility of that water,[3] how much more will holy water that has been consecrated by divine prayers be able to dispel the sterility of human things, to purge, clean, and sanctify whatever has been polluted, to multiply what is good, to overturn the snares of the devil, and defend human beings from the deceptions of demons? My brother priests, look to these examples and to others like them, and take care to fulfill this ministry entrusted to you with prayer, by the power of the Holy Spirit! The element of water about which we have spoken to you, and other substances which are apt for sacred uses and the treatment of human infirmities, you are hereby instructed to bless. Minister to the sick and perform diligently all other duties which pertain to your calling."

Guido [of Arezzo] states in his *On Music* that there are some demons who are not able to tolerate the sound of melody. In his work *On Antiquity*, [Flavius] Josephus relates that in the army of Titus there was a certain man who was able to expel demons from the bodies of possessed person by means of a stone set in a ring. He says also that a certain exorcist was able to expel demons by using some adjurations of Solomon and applying the roots of particular herbs to the nostrils of the possessed person, and that he witnessed this for himself. And there are many other learned teachers who attest to the effectiveness of such things, and their testimony cannot be dismissed without pride and presumption.

But it is important to note that, although there are many such examples, they are all dependent ultimately on the power of God, working through the exorcists of His holy Church. For in the various things created by God,

---

[3] See 2 Kings 2:12.

there is infused a certain power which comes from God Himself. This includes the powers of liberating those who are vexed by demons, and also of constraining the demons themselves and expelling them from the bodies of those whom they have possessed.

The explanation for this is as follows. Almighty God is the avenger of all evils. He punishes demons in a manner which befits them. Some of them He makes subject to the effects of various things of the senses. But this is not in any way contrary to His own divine power, since all corporeal and physical things have their own strength and virtue through what He has bestowed upon them. This is fully consistent with what we read concerning the punishment of the damned in hell, in Matthew 25, where it states that the souls of the damned, together with demons, will be tormented by fire—which is a physical substance.

The reason for this is that those who sin against God Himself and are unrepentant deserve the greatest possible penalty. But there is no penalty greater than the pain caused by the objects of the senses—in this case, fire.

Hence it can be concluded that the objects of the senses (including holy water, incense, herbs, musical sounds) are able to assist those afflicted by demons, in accordance with what the angel Raphael stated in the book of Tobit. This conclusion is also stated by the authors of the *Malleus Maleficarum*.[4] The authors of that work note that a certain herb called *hypericon*,[5] also known as 'flight-of-demons,' has great efficacy is repelling demonic attacks. Another example of this is the herb *rue*.[6] When this herb is applied to a possessed person, the unclean spirits cannot tolerate it. This

---

[4] The *Malleus Maleficarum* ('Hammer of Witches') is a classic treatise on witchcraft, written by Fr. Heinrich Kramer, OP, a German inquisitor, in the 15th century.

[5] i.e. St John's wort.

[6] A type of bitter herb.

is something which we ourselves have witnessed on an almost daily basis.

The reason for the effectiveness of such things is that, whereas demons delight in certain sensory objects, they are disturbed and deeply adverse to the presence of others. The things which disturb demons are typically those which cause genuine joy, wholesome strength, health, and virtue in human beings. But they delight in things which induce melancholy, weakness, and doubt in human beings—such as darkness, shadows, caves, places of desolation, and so forth. For in such places, they can work more freely and effectively. And thus it happens that human beings who spend much time in such environments are generally more prone to the vexations of demons.

Often a change of environment is in itself sufficient to dispel the vexations of demons; so that, if a person who is afflicted by demons or by witchcraft with melancholy or depression and customarily dwells in places of darkness, enclosure, and shadow, is brought into a situation of light and warmth (or other conditions conducive to joy), the demonic affliction or witchcraft ceases to afflict them.

Considering all of these cases, it is clear that priests and exorcists are indeed able to apply objects of the senses to alleviate the vexations of those possessed or afflicted by demons, or who are under the influence of a curse or spell. All such objects and material should be blessed beforehand, in the name of the Most Holy Trinity—the Father, the Son, and the Holy Spirit. Having such blessed objects and materials in the vicinity of the body of a person who is possessed will often cause the demons who are present to react is some way, such as by releasing a foul or bitter odor, or laughing, or something else. In these cases, the exorcist ought to continue with the application of the blessed material, so as to irritate and vex the demon. This not only reveals the presence of the demons, but also make it more likely that they will depart. The exorcist may also direct condemnatory, disapproval, and even derisive language to a demon in order to irritate it.

The reason that demons will cause the possessed person to laugh inappropriately or to make some other abnormal action is so that they prevent the possessed person from listening attentively to the word of God, which may inspire the possessed person to an act of prayer. Such things irritate the evil pride of demons and offend them greatly. This, in turn, induces them to depart.

It cannot be objected that we ought not to offend or curse any being by God deliberately. For the exorcist does not, in fact, do any injury to the demon (which remains a creation of God) out of mere hatred or malice. Rather, whatever irritations are inflicted on demons are done out of love of God, against whom the demon has rebelled; and also out of charity towards one's neighbor, for demons are foes to human beings during the course of this life. It is therefore licit to use insulting or derisive language against a demon, insofar as this contributes to revealing its presence or inducing it to cease afflicting a human being.

CHAPTER IV

HOW THE EXORCIST SHOULD QUESTION AND COMMAND THE DEMONS CONCERNED

AN EXORCIST is licitly able to question demons who have taken control of human bodies, in imitation of the example of Christ, who questioned such demons. For example, He asked: "What is your name?", as is found in Matthew 5. But the exorcist should be very careful that, in asking questions, he does not become a mere curious investigator. For it is not permissible to question demons except on matters which pertain directly to their expulsion from persons or objects of which they have taken possession, or which pertain to preventing harm they may cause, either to oneself or to one's neighbor.

Therefore, the exorcist must exercise the utmost caution in asking questions. For in asking any superfluous question, an avenue of deception is opened for the demon concerned. The exorcist, acting on the part of Christ, is able to interrogate the demon [or demons] only with the intention of gaining authority over it and power to expel it.

Pertinent and permissible questions thus include:
- whether they are many or few
- what its name is and what are the names of its companions
- why they have taken possession of this particular person and when they did so
- through which person or by which saint they are able to be expelled most readily
- who their particular enemies are, either among the angels and saints in heaven, or among the demons in hell
- which sacred words brings them the most discomfort or repulsion
- whether they are bound by any pact or work of witchcraft and, if so, how these may be annulled or rendered void
- who is their leader within the person of whom they have taken possession
- whether or not the person in question is genuinely possessed or afflicted by them.

These matters all pertain directly to the expulsion of the demon [or demons] in question, and are therefore permissible.

It is also permissible to threaten the demons who have taken possession of the person that, by the power and will of God, they shall be tortured by Lucifer and other infernal powers if they refuse to obey the exorcist. The minions of hell may be directed, in the virtue of God, to take away and punish a fellow demon who is possessing a person and who refuses to obey the exorcist. It is also permissible to command the principal demon (if a number of them have taken possession of a person) that he must take with him all of his companions.

For although demons agree among themselves in their intention and purpose of harming human beings, in all other matters they are natural enemies to each other and fight among themselves. Therefore, one demon will freely castigate another, if ordered to do so in the name of God.

CHAPTER V

CERTAIN THINGS OF WHICH THE EXORCIST OUGHT TO
BEWARE, BOTH IN PUBLIC AND IN PRIVATE

THE EXORCIST ought to compel any demons who have taken possession of a person, either by exorcisms or by commands, that they profess and declare the truth of the Catholic faith. This practice is to be done both for the honor of God and for the edification of any witnesses who may be present. And the demons should be commanded to show reverence for God, by virtue of this truth. For example, the demon or demons may be directed [in the body of the possessed person] to genuflect and incline their head to the ground three times, in honor of the Most Holy Trinity of the Father, the Son and the Holy Spirit.

The exorcist should take great care in such matters that he does not deviate or sway from what he has initially commanded, even if there appears to be a prolonged delay in the demon's obedience to him, or even if the demon mocks his instructions. Rather, the exorcist should persist firmly and with unwavering determination. For if the exorcist is deterred from what he has commanded, the demon will see itself as having obtained victory over that person. And after this, it will be extremely difficult to compel it to any obedience at all.

The exorcist should also be cautious in the application of sensible objects, such as sacred relics. He should take the utmost care to ensure that they are, in fact, genuine holy articles, whether they be relics of saints, or fragments of the True Cross, or other such items. He should take this caution both for his own sake, and for the sake of other persons who are present, and only use such articles if he is confidently assured of their authenticity. For demons will often pretend to be in fear of such items, when they know perfectly well that they are not genuine at all; and, afterwards, they will then mock or treat scornfully the non-genuine sacred article. They do this in order to undermine people's faith in the sacraments and piety of the holy Roman Church. I myself have sometimes witnessed this very thing occur in astonishing fashion.

CHAPTER VI

THE PERSEVERANCE AND PATIENCE WHICH THE EXORCIST
OUGHT TO POSSESS, AND THE REASONS WHY SOME DEMONS
CANNOT BE MADE TO DEPART

A N EXORCIST ought to have the very greatest patience and perseverance in any admonition or adjuration he issues to a demon. Above all, he should not despair of attaining victory over the foe, even if it happens that the demons he is dealing with are very persistent in their attacks and appear to refuse him.

For it should be known and understood that the commands given to a demon by a priest performing an exorcism are, in fact, the commands of God. If God so wished, by His power any demon could be put to flight easily and without resistance. Yet God does not always do this. Rather, He brings each matter to its conclusion in accordance with His will, at the time which He chooses. Although He has absolute power over demons, God determines when and how they obey Him.

This may be compared to the case of human beings, who are all necessarily obedient to the will of God, who is omnipotent. Yet often God does not immediately compel their obedience, but rather He encourages it through various means, such as through preaching, or through adversities and difficulties, and so forth. So it is that God uses exorcists to urge demons to cease their possession and vexation of human beings. The exorcists use words, prayers, and objects of the senses in order to act as goads to the demons. This works in the same manner as blows or threats act upon human beings, to urge them to obedience. It is in this context that an exorcist may use insulting, offensive, or derisive language against demons in order to liberate a possessed person, as we have explained towards the end of Chapter III of this treatise.

And just as some human beings are more resistant or stubborn in the face of urging, and less heedful of the Word of God, so are some demons more resistant to the words of exorcists. Nevertheless, if a demon adamantly and finally refuses to submit to the exhortations and commands of an exorcist, God Himself will apply His own power to compel them, when He sees fit to do so.

It is God who bestows the authority to priests and exorcists to expel and adjure demons. Sometimes He permits the demons to disobey these, for reasons of His own which are unknown to others. Sometimes, for example, a demon will be able to refuse to give its name to an exorcist rightly commanding it to do so. This happens, however, only in accordance with the decision and judgment of God. For it may be that, for some unknown reason, it is expedient that it should not respond to the interrogations of the exorcist at that point.

CHAPTER VII

OFFERING THE EUCHARIST TO POSSESSED PERSONS, AGAINST THE POPULAR OPINION ON THE MATTER

A N EXORCIST ought to encourage a person who is besieged or vexed by a demon to receive frequently the most holy Sacrament of the Eucharist. This is contrary to a commonly held opinion that people vexed by demons or by work of witchcraft should not receive Holy Communion while under the influence of such malign forces.

How much this common opinion is different from the truth of the matter is shown by the opinion of St. John Cassian, in his *Conferences of the Desert Fathers* (*Conference 70*), who concurs with our opinion. He writes:

> We cannot recall a single instance of where the ancient fathers forbade Holy Communion to those who were vexed or possessed by evil spirits. Rather, they believed that, if it was

possible, it ought to be received by them frequently, even daily. For this Sacrament is conducive to the purgation and protection of the body and soul. And when a person receives it, any evil spirit inhabiting their body or trying to hide within them will be tormented as if by fire, and so will seek to flee from them. Recently, we witnessed a monk, Br. Andronicus, cured from demonic possession by this very means. But if a demon sees his victim separated from the Heavenly medicine of the Eucharist, he will become even bolder and more obstinate in his vexations and attacks.

But some may object that, before receiving the Most Holy Body and Blood of Christ, a person ought to ensure that they are able to consume the host and drink from the chalice in a worthy manner—and that a person besieged by a demon cannot possibly do this, since they do not possess the use of reason. To this we respond with the opinion of St. Thomas Aquinas, who writes:

> A person may be said to lack the use of reason in two senses. One way is when the person's use of reason is impaired, but not fully absent; in the same way, a person may be said to lack the sense of sight, when they simply have poor vision. Such people, whose reason is impaired but not wholly absent, are able to consider the Sacrament with a certain devotion; and the Sacrament should not be denied to them on the grounds that their reason is impaired. The other way in which people are said to lack the use of reason is when they are completely incapable of

thought or reason, and have been from birth. The Sacrament should not be given to such people, since they are completely unable to consider it with proper devotion. But a person who has previously had the use of reason, and for some reason it is impaired or rendered inoperative, will still have had proper devotion to the Eucharist at an earlier stage, and, on the basis of this devotion which they had when they were mentally competent, they may still be given the Sacrament, unless there is a fear that they will vomit it up.

If St. Thomas is here writing concerning infirmities of the mind, the same principle applies equally to those whose mental capacities are impaired by demonic vexation. The exception to this is if it is known that their vexation of possession is the result of some serious sin or crime. And if this is the case, during the person's intervals of lucidity when they have the full use of reason, they should be encouraged to repent and make a full confession of their sins. And once they are sacramentally absolved in the sight of God, they should then not be denied the divine Sacrament of the Eucharist.

The exorcist ought to exorcise and bless all things which are to be used by the person who is possessed or besieged by a demon, or under the control of some work of witchcraft. This includes plates, cutlery, drinking vessels, ointments, and so forth. The same applies to all things which are to be used to dispel a demon from a human body.

An exorcist should also make a diligent search in the place where a possessed or bewitched person resides, examining carefully all corners of rooms, and looking in beds, blankets, pillows, under doorways, and in all other places of the house. If any suspicious, sinister, or unexplained object is found, it should immediately be disposed of and destroyed, by burning them in a fire which has been blessed. In fact, it is expedient to dispose of the person's current bedding and clothing entirely, and to commence with new ones. Sometimes it is also useful for the person suffering from demonic vexation or the malign effects of witchcraft to move to a different place of residence.

CHAPTER VIII

AN EXPLANATION OF CERTAIN HEBREW AND GREEK TITLES OF GOD WHICH ARE USED IN EXORCISMS

C AUTION SHOULD be taken that the exorcist does not use in his exorcisms various names which are not understood by him. St. John Chrysostom asserts that such practices are greatly to be feared.[1]

In this present collection of exorcisms, we have included a number of names which will not be understood by many. Nevertheless, these are all holy and authentic names and titles of God. So that no one shall be perplexed or confused by these, I have decided to include an explanation of these here. By this means, the exorcist will be able to use the exorcisms which follow securely and without doubtfulness.

---

[1] In the late Middle Ages and early-Modern Era, the use of Hebrew and Greek words in a superstitious manner had become widespread. Hence Menghi is careful to demonstrate here that the use of Hebrew and Greek titles of God in exorcisms is not a superstitious or quasi-magical practice, if the names are used with understanding.

It should be noted that, according to St. Jerome, the first name of God is *El.* The translators of the Septuagint,[2] interpret this as meaning "Strong God." The second and third names of God are *Elohim* and *Eloa,* which are interpreted as "God Himself." The fourth name is *Sabaoth,* which is interpreted as "of virtues" or "of armies." The fifth name is *Elom,* which means "Most High." The sixth is *Efe heie,* which is found in the book of Exodus, where we read: "*I am* sent me."[3]

The seventh name of God is *Adonai,* which is translated as "Lord" generally. The eighth is *Ya,* which is applied to God alone, and is found as the last syllable of *Alleluia.* The ninth name of God is *Tetragrammaton,*[4] which the Hebrews give as *Jehovah,* and believe to be a name which cannot be spoken.

The tenth name is *Shaddai,* which the Hebrews use to indicate "the God of Heaven" according to the translation of Aquila.[5] We, however, opine that it means "Strong and Omnipotent."

There are, beyond these, many names of God which are not generally understood. Certain people hold the use of these names to be superstitious and deserving of condemnation. But, properly considered and understood, it is clear that they are nothing other than holy and proper designations or titles of God. Such names include *Hagios, Ho Theos, Ischiros,* and *Athanatos.*[6]

Paolo Ghirlando, in his tract on witchcraft, states that he has often discovered such words being used in spells and

---

[2] That is, the Greek version of the Old Testament, in general use by the time of Christ.

[3] Exodus 3:14.

[4] *Tetragrammaton,* meaning "four letters," signifies the four-letter Hebrew word for Jehovah/Yahweh.

[5] Aquila of Sinope made a literal translation of the Old Testament into Greek in the 2nd century. Both Origen and St. Jerome made use of this translation.

[6] These are all Greek terms and are used as designations or descriptions of God. They mean, respectively, "Holy," "The God," "Strong," and "Immortal."

charms.[7] He further states that these are to be identified with *Deus Acharon*. But this name, *Acharon*, is in fact a name of Satan or Beelzebub. For this reason, he asserts that the use of the Greek names listed above are to be regarded as superstitious and wrong. How far this view is removed from the truth is clear from the fact that the Holy Roman Catholic Church uses these very words in the prayers offered on Good Friday and Holy Saturday, when it implores mercy from God for all the world.[8] Now, if the use of these words was actually superstitious, then the Church would not only refrain from using them, but would condemn them. I am astonished that such an upright, prudent, and learned man would have overlooked this, when it is obvious to the eyes of all, and especially clear to the faithful!

There are also various other names which are not understood by all people. An example is *Soter*, which is a Greek word meaning "Savior." For the Hebrews, there is the name *Jehovah*, which they regard as a word which cannot be pronounced, and which is the great name of God, and is discussed in the book *On the Holy Name of Jesus* by Arcangelo Da Borgonovo.[9] Its meaning can also be found in the work *Contra Hebraeos* by Pietro Colonna Galatino. *Agla* is another Hebrew word which is included among the names of God, which means "You are God, powerful throughout eternity."

---

[7] The author is referring here to a widely circulated tract on witchcraft, *Sententia de Sortilegiis*, by Paolo Ghirlando, an Italian lawyer. These Greek titles or description of God were often used in a superstitious manner by practitioners of witchcraft. Nevertheless, this does not negate their value when their true meaning is understood and intended.

[8] In the Tridentine Good Friday liturgy, Greek titles of God are used during the adoration of the cross: *Agios o theos. Agios ischyros. Agios athanatos, eleison imas.* These are also included in the Roman Missal of the Novus Ordo.

[9] Arcangelo Da Borgonovo was a Franciscan friar of the 16th century, who wrote on the mystical significance of the name of Jesus. He argues that this holy name is identical with the Tetragrammaton, or the unpronounceable name of God of the Hebrews.

Homousion is a Greek title which means "consubstantial," and is attributed to Christ, for He is consubstantial with the Father and the Holy Spirit.

Eheye is a Hebrew title and signifies the simple essence of the divinity of God.

CHAPTER IX

AN EXPLANATION OF CERTAIN LATIN TITLES OF GOD
WHICH THE AUTHOR HAS INCLUDED IN THE EXORCISMS

I N THE EXORCISMS contained in this work, there are certain Latin names and titles of God, taken from the Sacred Scriptures and the writings of the Church Fathers, and various people have attempted to identify the sources of these designations. So that they may be used with confidence and understanding by each exorcist who employs these exorcisms, I have decided to identify the origin of these names and titles of God here myself.[1]

"Alpha," "Omega," "First," "Last," "Beginning," and *"End"* are all to be found in Revelation 1.

In John 4, we read: "I know that the *Messiah* comes, who will be called *Christ."*

---

[1] In the citations which follow, the Latin titles of God which are employed in the exorcisms are all indicated in italics, with capital letters.

In Luke 2, we read: "His name shall be called *JESUS.*"

In John 18, we read: "It is you who say, '*King*'." And the Church very often uses the title of "*King*" in its hymns and acclamations.

The name "*Emmanuel*" is found in Isaiah 7, where we read: "Behold, a virgin will conceive and bear a Son, and His name shall be called '*Emmanuel*'." And in the great antiphons of Advent, the Church acclaims Christ as "Emmanuel and Lawgiver."

In John 8, we read: "I am the *Light* of the world."

In Mark 6: "When you pray, say '*Father*'."

In John 13: "You call me *Lord* and *Master*, and rightly so, for indeed I am."

John 8: "The *Beginning*—that is, I who speak these words to you."

In the letter of St. Paul to the Colossians, 2, we read: "He is the *Image* of the invisible God."

In John 10: "I am the *Sheepfold.*"

In John 14: "I am the *Way*, the *Truth*, and the *Life*."

In Luke 7: "A great *Prophet* has arisen among us."

In Corinthians 10: "The *Rock* was Christ."

In John 15: "I am the true *Vine*."

In Isaiah 22 and Revelation 3 and in the fourth of the great Advent antiphons, Christ is referred to as the *Key*.

In Luke 1: "The *Virtue* of the Most High shall overshadow you."

In Luke 2: "She gave birth to her *Firstborn* Son."

In Isaiah 26: "Send for the *Lamb*, the Lord of the earth." And in Isaiah 53: "Like a *Lamb* in the presence of its shearers..." And in Jeremiah 11 and 51: "Like a meek *Lamb*, led as a sacrifice..."

In Psalm 18: "Like a *Bridegroom* coming forth from His chamber…"

In Genesis 1, God is given the title of *Creator*, where we read: "In the beginning, God *created* Heaven and earth." And the Church addresses God as *Creator* in the hymns: "O God, *Creator* of all;" and "O Come, *Creator* Spirit."

Similarly, the Church very often addresses Christ as *Redeemer*, such as in the hymn "Christ, *Redeemer* of all."

In John 12, Christ takes to Himself the title of *Shepherd:* "I am the good *Shepherd.*"

In Luke 5, we find the title *Teacher*: "*Teacher*, we have been laboring throughout the night and have caught nothing."

In Hebrews 1, Christ is referred to as *Splendor*: "He is the *Splendor* of His glory and the figure of His substance." And in her hymns, the Church acclaims: "You are the light, You are the *Splendor* of the Father;" and "To You, O Christ, *Splendor* of the Father."

In 2 Timothy 4, we read: "The Lord, as a just *Judge*, will repay everyone on that day."

In Proverbs 9: "*Wisdom* has built herself a home." And in 1 Corinthians 1: "He has become for us *Wisdom*." And the Church sings in the first of the great Advent antiphons, speaking to Christ: "O *Wisdom*, who have proceeded from the mouth of the Most High."

In Malachi 4, we read: "The *Sun* of justice will arise upon those fearing My name." And the Church, in one of its antiphons addressed to the Blessed Virgin Mary, acclaims: "Out of you is born the *Sun* of justice."

In Revelation 22, we read: "I am the *Root* of David, and the splendid *Morning Star*." In Isaiah 11: "And a *Flower* shall spring up from his root."

The Church, in its liturgy, proclaims Christ with the designation of *Priest*: "The eternal *Priest*, Christ the Lord." And in Hebrews 4, we encounter: "He was given by God the title of *High Priest* of the order of Melchizedek."

In 1 John 4, it is stated that: "God is *Love*."

The title of *Only Begotten* is found in 1 John 1: "God so loved the world that He gave His *Only-Begotten* Son."

In John 5: "The *Paraclete*, the Holy Spirit whom the Father will send..." And the Church sings: "You who are called *Paraclete*."

In 1 Timothy 2: "There is one *Mediator* for men, the man Jesus Christ."

"*God*," "*Eternal*," and "*Almighty*" are obviously divine titles which are used constantly by the Church.

In 1 Corinthians 1, we encounter: "But we preach Christ, the *Virtue* of God." And in the same place, we read: "But for us who are to be saved, He is the *Virtue* of God."

In John 6, we find the title of *Bread* being applied by Christ to Himself: "I am the *Bread* of life."

The Church assigns to Christ the title of *Healing*, when it sings, "You come as the *Healing* of the world."

In Revelation 5, we read: "The *Lion* of the tribe of Judah has conquered."

In Luke 2, Christ is declared to be: "The *Light* (*lumen*) for the illumination of the nations."

In Isaiah 25, He is given the title of *Mouth:* "The *Mouth* of the Lord has spoken."

In John 1, He is designated by the title *Word:* "In the beginning, was the *Word*," and "The *Word* was made flesh."

In Isaiah 6: "*Holy, Holy, Holy* Lord, God of hosts."

In Revelation 4: "Holy, Lord God, *Omnipotent*."

In Exodus 34: "Ruler, Lord *Merciful* God." In Jonah 4: "Because You are God, clement and *Merciful*." In James 5: "You have seen that the Lord is *Merciful*."

In 1 Timothy 1: "To the King of the Ages, *Immortal*." And the Church acclaims God as: "Holy, strong, and *Immortal*."

The Church proclaims Christ as *Peace-Maker King*: "He is the *Peace-Maker King*." She proclaims Him also as the *Dawn*, in the fifth of the great Advent antiphons: "O *Dawn*, splendor of the eternal light and Sun of Justice."

Christ is given the designation *Goodness* also by the Church when she addresses Him thus: "Christ, true light, *Goodness* and life." The *Highest Good* is also used as a divine designation, such as by the Master of Sentence [Peter Lombard], who writes: "God made the rational creature, so that it might understand the *Highest Good*; and by understanding, love; and by loving, possess; and by possessing, enjoy."

Hope is used as a divine title in Psalm 13, "For the Lord is his *Hope*," and in Psalms 90 and 141, "You, O Lord, are my *Hope.*"

Honor is used as a divine appellation by the Church in the office of the Holy Trinity, in which it proclaims: "Our hope and our *Honor*, O blessed Trinity!"

The title of *Spirit* is frequently used, such as in John 4: "God is a *Spirit.*"

CHAPTER X

AN EXPLANATION OF CERTAIN TITLES OF THE BLESSED VIRGIN MARY WHICH ARE INCLUDED IN SOME OF THE EXORCISMS

BECAUSE MANY have requested that the sources and authorities of the various titles given to the Blessed Virgin Mary be identified, we have resolved to do this here, whether the titles originate from Sacred Scripture, or from the writings of the saints, or from the prayers and liturgy of the Church. This will allow exorcists to use these titles with more confidence and understanding.

We shall begin with the first title, identifying its sources, and then do the same for those which follow.

Virgin
Isaiah 7: "Behold, a *Virgin* shall conceive."
The prayer of the Church: "The *Virgin* Mary was assumed…" "O clement, O loving, O sweet *Virgin* Mary."

Mary
Luke 1: "Hail *Mary*, full of grace."
Matthew 1: "When the Mother of Jesus, *Mary*, was betrothed to Joseph."
Luke 2: "*Mary* treasured all these words in her heart."

Mother of Our Lord Jesus Christ
Obviously, the Gospels very frequently identify Mary as the Mother of Christ.

Queen
The antiphons of the Church: "*Queen* of Heaven, rejoice!"; "Hail, *Queen* of Heaven."

Glorious and *Lady*[1]
In the hymn of the Church: "O *Glorious Lady*."

Dawn
Song of Songs 4: "Who is this, who approaches like the rising *Dawn*?"

Handmaid
Luke 1: "Behold, the *Handmaid* of the Lord."

Garden and *Font*
Song of Songs 6: "An enclosed *Garden*, a sealed *Font*."

Well
Song of Songs 6: "A *Well* of living water."

Moon and Sun
Song of Songs 6: "Beautiful as the *Moon*, radiant as the *Sun*."

---

[1] The Latin word here is *Domina*, customarily rendered in English as "Lady."

Door
Ezekiel 44: "This _Door_ shall be closed to sin."
The hymn of the Church: "O happy _Door_ of Heaven."

Blessed
Luke 1: "You are _Blessed_, for you have believed…"
The antiphon of the Church: "_Blessed_ are you, Virgin Mary, for you merited to bear the Lord, the Creator of the world."

Loving[2]
The Church in its antiphon: "O clement, O _Loving_, O sweet Virgin Mary."

Bush
An antiphon of the Church: "The _Bush_, which Moses saw to be unburnt…"

Doorway
A hymn of the Church: "You are the _Doorway_ of the great King, and the portal of resplendent light."

Star
A hymn of the Church: "Hail, O _Star_ of the Sea."

Tower
Song of Songs 7: "Your neck is like a _Tower_ of ivory."

Beautiful (Pulchra)
Song of Songs 6: "You are _Beautiful_, my beloved!"

Beloved and _Lovely (Formosa)_
Song of Songs 6: "Come my _Beloved_, my _Lovely_ one, come!"

---

[2] The Latin word here is _pia_, which could also be rendered as 'merciful.'

Beautiful (Speciosa)
The Church in its antiphon: "You were created *Beautiful* and sweet."

Veil
St. Bernard, in his Sermon 8 on the Assumption: "Mary is a *Veil* between Christ and the Church."

Beloved (Alma)
In the antiphon of the Church: "*Beloved* Mother of the Redeemer."

Flower
Sons of Songs 3: "I am the *Flower* of the field."

Other titles of the Blessed Virgin Mary, similarly well authorized by Scripture, the liturgy of the Church, and the writings of the Church Fathers, include:

Theotokos, Tabernacle, Arc, Bridal chamber, Hall, Cloud, Pearl, Ladder, Empress, etc.

CHAPTER XI

WHETHER THE EXORCIST SHOULD USE NOTES OR CARDS
WITH TEXT, AND THE RULES FOR DOING THIS LICITLY, AND
GENERAL CRITERIA FOR DETERMINING WHETHER A
PRACTICE IS SUPERSTITIOUS OR LICIT

I T IS PERMISSIBLE for an exorcist to use notes or cards, containing various holy names and words to be used in exorcisms. Such cards can, in fact, also be physically applied to the possessed person in order to remove their affliction, but this must be done with discretion and prudence, for it can be done either licitly or in a superstitious way.

There are a number of general rules for discerning if this practice (or any other) is conducted properly, rather than as an illicit superstition.

The first rule is that the glory of God should be the primary objective and goal of the undertaking. Indeed, this should be the case with all human work. The human mind and will must be brought into subjection to God, and seek His glory in all that is done; just as we read in 1 Corinthians

10: "Whether you eat or drink, or doing anything at all, do it for the glory of God."

The second rule for judging whether something is superstitious or not is whether its aims are restraining the flesh, or promoting some form of physical work, in a manner which is consistent with the rites and practices of the Catholic Church and the moral doctrine of the Church Fathers.

The third consideration or rule is whether the practice is or is not consistent with the practices of the universal Church, or the teaching of Sacred Scripture (as interpreted by the Church), or, at the very least, consistent with a well-established practice of a particular local Church, or a generally accepted and approved custom. This last consideration (of general and accepted custom) is, according to St. Augustine, to be considered as having legal force.[1]

St. Gregory the Great, writing upon this point to St. Augustine of Canterbury (who was working as a missionary to the English), comments: "There are different customs of the Church in the celebration of Masses. To me, it seems that whether the customs of Rome, or France, or whatever other local Church, are followed depends entirely upon which will give glory to God more effectively."[2] St. Thomas Aquinas also writes: "Certain variances in customs of the local Church are not incompatible with the Divine truth."

The fourth consideration in determining whether a practice is licit or superstitious is whether or not it accords with the proper order of nature, as ordained by God. The principle is applied in physics, medicine, and the astronomical sciences, but is no less applicable to questions of theology and morals.

---

[1] This is also a general principal of Roman law and Canon law, namely, that if a practice or procedure is established by custom it is to be considered licit, in the absence of specific legislation to the contrary.

[2] St. Gregory is here referring to minor variances in the liturgical practices of the Latin rite from one nation to another which existed at his time.

The fifth rule for determining whether a practice is licit or superstitious is the question of whether it gives rise to any scandal, or gives rise to harm to one's fellow man. However, it is to be noted that if an action or practice is the cause of a certain surprise or shock (akin to scandal) among the faithful, it does not always mean that it is superstitious or illicit. But it does mean that it should preferably be avoided, or at least not conducted publicly.

If any action or practice breaks any of the rules given above, it is to be regarded as superstitious and sinful.

On account of the first rule given above (that all things should be done for the glory of God), a practice like literally following the instructions of the Old Testament, or even some of the counsels of the New Testament, in cases where they are contrary to the teachings or practices of the Roman Church, would be considered superstitious.[3]

The second principle would apply if a person foolishly refused to do basic chores on a Saturday, or if they wished to fast on Sundays. These, and other such intentions, are to be judged as superstitious, because they are not in accordance with the teachings or customs of the Church. An exception would be if a person took up fasting on Saturday out of devotion to the Blessed Virgin Mary.

An example of a superstitious practice against the third rule or principle given above would be the use of particular rites or ceremonies (such as processions) which do not conform themselves to either the universal practice of the Church or to any accepted local Church custom.

An example of a superstitious practice in violation of the fourth rule given above would be the use of unknown names, characters, or symbols, whose supposed workings have nothing to do with the order of nature, or which do not express some prayer or invocation of the power of God.

---

[3] An example of this might be commending "hating one's father and mother" (Luke 14:26) in a literal sense; since this would not be in accord with established Church practice, and therefore not to the glory of God.

Examples of such things would be rings, stones, and amulets carved with astrological symbols or unknown words. Another example of this type of superstition would be the belief that the influence of the Heavens or the stars determines human actions.

The fifth rule, concerning the possibility of generating scandal, means that even some blessings of the sick (which are perfectly orthodox) should be conducted only privately.

All those who wish to conduct exorcisms with propriety ought to follow each of these five rules given above for avoiding anything superstitious.

In addition, there are *seven other conditions*, laid down by St. Thomas Aquinas. All blessings and exorcisms are, of course, to be done by virtue of the Divine Name, or the Blood of Christ, or some other holy and sacred power.

The first condition is that the exorcist should ensure that there are no words which imply an invocation of demonic powers, either expressly or implicitly.

The second condition is that the exorcist should not use any names or words which are not understood, at least by the exorcist himself.[4] According to St. John Chrysostom, such words are to be carefully avoided, lest any superstition may be hidden within them.

The third condition is that no element of falsehood should be contained in any of the words of exorcism employed. Indeed, anything containing falsehood cannot be expected to attain any result from God, for He is Himself a witness to the truth. Many old women fall into this practice, foolishly using falsehoods in an attempt to attain results.[5]

---

[4] This important condition is addressed in the author's explanation of the Hebrew, Greek, and Latin names employed in the exorcisms in this volume. See Chapter VIII.

[5] It is not precisely clear what the author is referring to here. Perhaps an example would be the identification of something non-genuine as a holy relic,

The fourth condition is that no vain or superstitious symbols be employed, except for those of genuine piety and meaning, such as the sign of the cross.

The fifth condition is that no faith should be placed simply in a particular style of writing or script or other such consideration, where such things do not pertain to the matter at hand or are not done with the intention of divine reverence. To believe in the efficacy of such things must be regarded as a superstition.[6]

The sixth condition is that in the use of divine words, whether of prayers of or Sacred Scripture, proper attention is placed on the meanings and sense of the words themselves. All of them should be used with reverence for the power of God. If used without understanding and reverence, as if they were able to attain the desired result in and of themselves, their use can become superstitious. The same applies also to the use of relics of saints, where the assistance of God should be sought through the intercession of such saints.

The seventh condition is that the final outcome of whatever procedure is being used (whether it is an exorcism or blessing) should be understood as being left ultimately to the will of God and whatever is pleasing to Him. For it is God alone who knows and determines what should be granted to the one who is asking Him.

If all of these conditions are observed, it is permissible and proper to exorcize those who are suffering from demonic possession or vexation, and to use cards or notes with sacred words inscribed upon them, either to be worn from their neck or simply carried on their person.

---

or making a promise or vow with no intention of keeping it. The word *vetulae*, translated here as "old women," was also sometimes use to indicate witches.

[6] An example of this would be the belief that if certain words were said in Latin, Greek, or Hebrew, they will produce an effect in a quasi-magical fashion.

CHAPTER XII

THE TRICKS AND CUNNING PLOYS OF DEMONS, AND CERTAIN
REMEDIES TO THESE

A N EXORCIST ought to be aware of certain tricks
and cunning ploys often employed by demons
who have taken possession of human bodies, so
as to avoid being deceived or taken in by these. Although
the variety of these tricks is virtually infinite, I shall here
describe some of the more commonly encountered or typical
occurrences.

Firstly, demons often attempt to conceal their presence
from the exorcist completely, and thus to avoid speaking or
making any motions. If they are unable to do this, then they
will then often attempt to display themselves as being very
strong and fearless in the presence of the priest, in the hope
that he will be less confident of victory against them.

A demon, if forced to speak by the exorcist by the
power of divine words, will often speak only interiorly to
the mind of the possessed person, rather than audibly so

that the exorcist may hear. This is part of an attempt to conceal its presence from the exorcist. If the exorcist suspects that this is happening, he should instruct the possessed person to reveal to him whatever the demon is saying interiorly to them. The exorcist may also adjure the demon to speak in a manner which is audible to him as well.

If the demon has been compelled to speak openly by the exorcist, it will often resist this by attempting to confuse the mind of the possessed person, so that whatever is said or read to that person is not clearly grasped. It may also attempt to disturb or confuse the exorcist or disrupt the procedure, by means of flippant or facetious words, or crying, or making jokes and jests with other people present. The exorcist should be aware when this begins to take place, and should adjure the demon, by the power of God, to desist from whatever such actions or words it may be employing.

It often happens that when it is a woman who is being exorcized—especially a young woman—the demon will cause her to feel, or to feign, some womanly illness or other indisposition. Then the exorcist will, in order to examine and assess her condition, be induced to make physical contact with her (such as by touching her face), or come into closer physical proximity to her. Through this device, the demon attempts to arouse feelings of carnal lust, either in the exorcist himself or in the victim of the possession. For this reason, the exorcist should exercise great caution in responding to anything which seems to demand physical contact and physical proximity with such subjects, and should carefully guard his senses (including sight and touch) against any occasions for lust.

If happens not infrequently that when a demon is adjured by the exorcist to state its name, it does so; but it will refuse to disclose the names of its confederate demons. It may perhaps claim that it cannot do so, because God does not will it, because the names of its associates are unspeakably foul. Sometimes this may indeed be true, but often it is false.

If it happens that if a demon claims it is unable to disclose the names of it associates, the exorcist should therefore specifically adjure the demon to speak truthfully in making its reply. If, after this, the principal demon is still unable to speak the names of its associates, it should then be ordered to give the other demons (its associates) the opportunity to speak for themselves, and then these should be commanded to give their names. And if these are unwilling to do so for fear of their superior, it should also be commanded not to inhibit them from doing this in any way.

But if it happens that the exorcist is unable to gain knowledge of the names of the demons concerned, he should address each one by some derisive appellation, for the sake of identification. For example, he might call the principal demon *Fachinus*, and the second *Pistor* and the third *Coquus Achernotis*, and other such titles.[1]

The exorcist should be aware also that when demons sense that they are not able to prevail against him or that they are losing ground against him, they are then likely to summon further associates to their aid. They do this in much the same way that a human being would call upon others to help him in a time of difficulty or trouble. Often this is done in a hidden or concealed manner. To guard himself against such an eventuality, the exorcist should be ready to invoke the intercession and virtues of further saints to his own aid. He should also explicitly prohibit the demon from calling further demonic companions to its presence.

Often when a demon is beginning to fail against the power of an exorcism, it will flee from the mouth or head of the possessed person and conceal itself in their lower members or interior parts. If this happens, the exorcist

---

[1] These names signify respectively "Bag-carrier," "Flour-grinder," and "Cook of Acheron" (i.e. Hell).

should attempt to retain the demon in the upper parts of the possessed person, so that the interrogation of the demon may continue, and so that it may not evade the power of the exorcism. As a remedy to this strategy, the exorcist should make the sign of the cross on the forehead or head of the possessed person, saying: "Behold the cross of the Lord! Flee, O demon, from the nether parts of this person." Or the exorcist may recite the psalm: "How long, O Lord, will You forget me until the end."[2] Even if this involves making a temporary stop in the prayer of exorcism, the exorcist should call the demon back to the upper parts of the afflicted person.

Different demons are afflicted more by different sacred words and signs, and some demons will be brought to obedience more promptly by some than others. For this reason, even after the principal demon or demons have been expelled, some other demons may remain within the person. When this occurs, it very often happens that the remaining demons call back the ones who were expelled, and thus the person returns to their former state. For this reason, the exorcist should always take care to command the demons that, after having left the departed person, they are never to return.

If this is not done, it often happens that the expelled demons re-enter the person whom they formerly possessed, just as the Savior says.[3] And they can do this with the slightest opportunity, even through venial sins. For this reason, any person who has been liberated from demonic possession through an exorcism should maintain assiduous prayer and attentiveness to their faith and actions for several months afterwards. They should receive holy Communion frequently, and at least on feast days. If they are married, they may (with the agreement of their spouse)

---

[2] Psalm 12:1.
[3] See Matthew 12:43-45.

practice sexual continence for a period of time. If this last counsel is not possible, they should at least take care not to initiate sexual contact for a period of time.

Often demons who have been expelled from a possessed person will try to persuade that person that they were never, in fact, really possessed at all. In this way they strive to weaken their feelings of gratitude towards God, and also to make them less cautious or less diligent in their piety.

For this reason, the exorcist should take care to instruct the liberated person that they should be persistent and sincere in their thanksgiving and devotions to God, and also that they should be on their guard against any temptations or demonic suggestions which they may encounter.

When the exorcist feels that he is gaining the upper hand in his task and that the demon or demons are starting to becoming afraid, he should warn the possessed person to ignore anything that the demons may say to them and not to listen to any of their suggestions.

As soon as a demon manifests some sign of its presence, the exorcist should begin to question it, if he has not done so already—even if this involves making a stop in the prayer of exorcism which he is reading.

He should question it, binding it to answer truthfully under adjuration by the virtue of God, asking:
-   who it is and who its associates are
-   the cause of it gaining entrance into the possessed person, and when this occurred
-   who are its particular foes, both in Heaven (among the saints and angels) and also in Hell (among its fellow demons)
-   its name and the names of its associates.

The names of both the principal demons and its associates should be carefully written down by the exorcist. Then they can be used accurately and consistently in commanding, questioning, or addressing them. Furthermore, if any of the demons are resistant to obeying the exorcist, he should write its name on a piece of paper and burn this in a fire that has been blessed. This is a procedure which demons find particularly tormenting; it shames and disconcerts them, for it reminds them of the flames of Gehenna.

Once the demon or demons have answered all these questions, the exorcist should then carefully confirm the veracity and the accuracy of all the answers he has received.

In interrogating demons, the exorcist must take care that he is in no way frivolous and that he asks nothing out of mere curiosity or anything superfluous to his task of liberating the victim from their affliction. If the exorcist should err in this respect and let motives of curiosity (or any other improper motives) enter into his questioning, it is possible that God will subtract the due obedience which the demons should give him.

When the exorcist has obtained answers to the relevant questions and has had these confirmed, he should then proceed with the exorcism. At the conclusion of each prayer of exorcism, he should question the demon or demons if they are now willing to depart. When a demon says it is wishing to depart from the possessed person, the exorcist should not immediately give it permission to do so, until it confirms that:

- it will take all of its companions with it when it leaves; and
- having departed from the person, it will never enter them again.

A firm promise from the demon should be obtained respecting these two conditions before the exorcist grants it leave to depart.

If an exorcist issues a command to a demon and finds that it does not obey him immediately, he should not immediately desist from what he has ordered. Rather, he should repeat his commands, adding (if appropriate) further adjurations, and be firmly insistent upon obedience. Above all, he should permit the demon no rest or respite from his commands and adjurations, whether this be through reading prayers of exorcism or direct commands.

He should also not permit himself to be engaged in any questioning or conversation with demons merely out of curiosity, as we have stated before. For when this happens, the fortitude and spirit of the priest is diminished, while the demon itself gains strength and energy.

Chapter XIII

Other Deceptions Which Demons Typically Use Against Exorcists, and of Which the Exorcist Must Be Aware

THERE ARE certain demons who have such an intense hatred of sacred words that even before an exorcism has commenced, they depart from the person whom they have possessed. There are others who wait for the exorcism to begin, but then find themselves unable to tolerate hearing sacred words spoken, and so leave very promptly.

On the other hand, there are some who are so evil and malignant that they remain persistently, strongly resisting the exorcist and doing their best to fatigue him. Some cause the afflicted person to appear to be ill rather than possessed. In these cases, the demon is trying to cause the exorcist to cease from his efforts, either through exhaustion and fatigue, or through deceit. If the exorcist does cease from his efforts, the demons then count this as a great victory for themselves—most especially when the exorcist is overcome with fatigue, or when he gives up out of despair of attaining success.

For this reason, it behooves the exorcist to be constant and untiring in his efforts, and not to let his faith or confidence fail him. Once he has commenced an exorcism, he should proceed persistently, until he can see clearly that the afflicted person has been liberated. Sometimes this involves continuous engagement in an exorcism for four hours, or even for six hours. If it happens that the demons appear to be more afraid of the exorcist in the first hour than in the second or subsequent hours, the exorcist should not be discouraged, because little by little their resistance will be worn down. If the possessed person is not liberated in the first hour, the exorcist should continue for a second hour, then a third, and so forth; persisting until the person has been definitely liberated from their demonic affliction.

As has been noted, certain demons try to make it seem like the possessed person is only suffering from a natural or physical ailment. Others try to make it seem like the demonic possession or vexation is not real at all, but only something being feigned by the person concerned.

In some cases, the demons will cause the possessed person to fall asleep in the course of the exorcism. They may also cause the possessed person to have certain visions, such as of the crucified Christ or certain saints. All of this is done to disrupt the course of the exorcism and prevent it from coming to a fruitful conclusion.

Sometimes demons will conceal themselves within the body of the possessed person, so that they will seem to be free of their possession.

Sometimes demons will try to persuade the person whom they have possessed or afflicted that the exorcist is practicing some form of witchcraft on them, and that the exorcism is an illicit or superstitious procedure. The exorcist should be wary of this; and, at the same time, avoid anything which is, or may appear to be, superstitious.

An exorcist should not be surprised if a person who regularly receives the sacrament of Holy Communion becomes possessed. Although the reception of the Blessed Sacrament disturbs and repels demons, it is possible that a demon may enter someone who regularly receives the Eucharist at a time when it is no longer within their system.

Certain demons even speak of the mysteries of our Faith and the Divine Majesty to the person they have possessed, with the intention of generating scruples or excessive fastidiousness in them. They do this in order to disturb and weaken their victim, and to make them reluctant (because of this scrupulosity) to receive the Blessed Sacrament.

Some demons, after a long possession of a particular person, begin to speak and act through them constantly—in other words, to take over their victim's whole personality, to such a point that it seems like the person is no longer being harmed or disturbed at all. The demon will then begin to vex them again only after it has been detected and the exorcist begins proceedings against it.[1]

---

[1] This last observation has been paraphrased somewhat from the original Latin text, for the sake of clarity.

CHAPTER XIV

OTHER THINGS OF WHICH THE EXORCIST MUST BE AWARE IN CURING THOSE POSSESSED BY DEMONS OR UNDER THE INFLUENCE OF WITCHCRAFT

THE EXORCIST ought to endeavor to gain knowledge of all matters pertaining to the subject of an exorcism. This includes how the demon gained entrance into the possessed person, and also whether or not the person concerned is under the influence of any witchcraft or spells.

The exorcist should know the signs which help to distinguish whether an afflicted person is possessed by a demon or under the influence of witchcraft, or both. He should be familiar with the signs which possessed persons exhibit when exorcism proceedings are commenced with them, and he should also recognize the means by which a demon departs from the body of a possessed person. Further, as we have noted, he ought to be cognizant of the malicious tricks and subterfuges which demons employ in order to deceive exorcists.

We have spoken of some of these above, and will speak further of them in our *Cudgel of Demons*, Chapters 11, 12 and 13.[1]

---

[1] These chapters are included as an Appendix to this volume.

CHAPTER XV

THE PLACE AND TIME WHEN EXORCISMS SHOULD BE UNDERTAKEN

THE EXORCIST should take care, unless there is no practical alternative, to avoid carrying out his duties in private houses, lest occasion of scandal is given to the small-minded. Rather, exorcisms should preferably be carried out in churches or chapels, or other such places specially dedicated to God.

The reason for this is that in private houses there are often persons present who are susceptible to the influence of demons, as well as various objects and items which are spiritually impure, or at the very least secular and worldly. Churches and chapels are the proper places assigned to sacred actions. It is there that possessed persons ought to be exorcized, and there that solemn commands and adjurations are most effectively made against demons. In such consecrated places, demons will be more in fear of what is holy and of sacred words than in other locations, since each church or chapel is a house of prayer and a dwelling-place of God. It is in such sacred places that our prayers and deprecations will be heard and received most readily by God.

Regarding the times at which exorcisms are to occur, this is not specified or determined. According to what charity requires, so may exorcisms be performed at any time. It will generally be most effective and appropriate, however, for exorcisms to be conducted in the mid-morning, after the celebration of the Holy Mass. Again, it is often found that exorcisms are more powerful and efficacious on days of greater holiness and sacred solemnity, such as the Solemnities of the Nativity, Resurrection and Ascension of Our Lord, the feast of Pentecost, and other such days. Also, exorcisms tend to be more effective and efficacious on feasts, or the vigils of the feasts, of the Blessed Virgin Mary, the apostles, and other significant holy festivities.

The exorcist must be cautious, however, that, notwithstanding the fact that such holy days may be especially conducive to procuring a good result, he should never undertake an exorcism hastily and unless he himself is well-prepared personally. This is especially so in respect to those elements described earlier in Chapter I of this work—namely, firmness of faith, purity of conscience, and humility.

CHAPTER XVI

AN EXPLANATION OF WHY EVEN RIGHTEOUS PERSONS ARE ABLE TO BE VEXED BY DEMONS

HERE ARE certain people who are surprised at the fact that even righteous and faithful persons sometimes are vexed by unclean spirits. They do not understand the causes for which our blessed God sometimes permits this to happen. Nor do they consider the conditions and factors which are granted by the will of God—namely, the knowledge and power possessed by demons, and also their ability to exercise their own free will. Demons employ these attributes in their workings. It is by virtue of these attributes of demons, which are granted and permitted to them by almighty God, that they are able to attack even persons of righteous life.

Demonic afflictions fall upon righteous persons not as a consequence of their sins or culpability, but rather simply as pains or sufferings. According to St. Thomas Aquinas, the sufferings of this life are not to be understood as the direct consequence of personal sin, for sometimes grievous sufferings full upon innocent persons. Rather, it happens in accordance with the wise but mysterious judgments and purposes of God, as we see in Aquinas's commentary on John 9.[1]

---

[1] This chapter includes the story of the cure of the man born blind, of whom it is asked whether it was his sins or those of his parents which caused his affliction. Christ replies that his blindness was not caused either by his own sins or the sins of his parents. John 9:3-2.

CHAPTER XVII

WHY CERTAIN POSSESSED PERSONS ARE NOT ABLE TO BE
LIBERATED FROM DEMONIC POSSESSION

I T IS TO BE NOTED that there are many who are possessed or besieged by demons who are not able to be successfully liberated from these unclean spirits. This happens only by the permission of God. When some people see this kind of situation, they are filled with astonishment, for they cannot imagine any reason why it should transpire. Because of this, we shall discuss the matter here. There are six reasons why it sometimes comes about that certain persons are not liberated from demonic possession, and all attempts to exorcize them prove to be unsuccessful. There is also a seventh reason we shall give, but on that seventh reason we make no conclusive judgment.

The first reason is the feebleness of faith on the part of those who surround the afflicted person, or the deficiency of the faith of the person themselves.[1] An example of this is to be found in the Gospel, in which the father of a boy possessed by a demon says to Our Lord: "I believe, Lord, help my unbelief." And then Jesus exclaims: "O generation of unbelievers, how much longer must I be with you?"[2]

The second reason is some grave sin on the part of the person possessed. In his commentary on the abovementioned incident, St. Jerome offers the opinion that the reason the boy was possessed so severely was possibly because of his own sins.

Thirdly, there are cases where there is a negligence or failure to apply the appropriate measures on the part of the exorcist. In the same case of the possessed boy mentioned above, whom the apostles were not able to be liberate from possession, as related in Matthew 17 and Mark 9, it is to be noted that the most powerful of the apostles, the Pillars of the Church, St. Peter, St. James, and St. John, were not present at the time.[3] Also, as St. John Chrysostom, observes, they had failed to apply the remedies of prayer and fasting which were necessary to exorcize that demon.[4]

The fourth reason is a failure or deficiency in the faith of the exorcist himself. In the incident mentioned above, when some disciples ask why they were unable to liberate the boy from possession, Christ replies to them: "Because you have so little faith. Truly I tell you, if you have faith as small as a mustard seed, you can say to this mountain, 'Move from here to there,' and it will move. Nothing will be impossible for you!'"[5] Of this, St. Hilary comments that the

---

[1] The text of this chapter has been restructured. In the original, the seven reasons are listed, and after that examples of each are given. For the sake of clarity, the examples have been stated immediately after each of the reasons named.

[2] See Matthew 17:14–20 and Mark 9:14–24.

[3] See Mark 9:14.

[4] See Mark 14:28–29.

[5] See Matthew 17:19–20.

disciples certainly believed, but their faith was still not sufficiently strong to produce the desired result.

The fifth reason that an attempted exorcism may not succeed is that it may provide the opportunity for the virtue of another person to achieve the desired result. We encounter an example of this in the *Lives of the Desert Fathers*, where we read of St. Anthony of Egypt not being able to cure certain persons from demonic possession, but his disciple, Paul, was able to do so.

The sixth reason why demonic possession or vexation is sometimes permitted to continue by God is that it may serve as a kind of purgation. Even when eternal remission for their sins has been obtained, the suffering resulting from demonic vexation serves as a kind of temporal penance, conducive to the full purgation of their souls.

The seventh reason is that trials of demonic affliction are permitted to be continued on account of some special merit or sanctity of the person concerned.[6]

---

[6] This seventh reason is the one for which the author offers no examples, and reserves his own opinion. There are many examples in the lives of saints where persons of particular sanctity and virtue are afflicted by demons. The reason for his reticence on this subject, however, is perhaps to guard against the view that demonic vexation is, in itself, a sign of outstanding sanctity or virtue.

Chapter XVIII

Whether Possessed Persons Should Be Exorcized Publicly or Privately, and the Benefits Which Come to the Faithful by Witnessing Exorcisms

THE EXORCIST ought to take care that during an exorcism he never remains alone with any female subject, whether this is in a church or in some private place. This even applies if the woman to be exorcized is very elderly. There are several reasons for this.

Firstly, demons often agitate human bodies to such an extent that unless there are others present who are able to restrain the person physically, the procedure becomes extremely difficult, if not impossible.[1]

Secondly, having an exorcist remain alone with a female subject can readily give cause to scandal and gossip.

---

[1] Since the author is speaking about female subjects of exorcism here, he is perhaps assuming that in the case of a male subject, the exorcist would be able to restrain him himself without scandal. Nevertheless, this reason would seem to be applicable to male subjects in many cases as well.

Thirdly, having other people present, especially if they are praying devoutly for the suffering person, can bring about a successful result for the exorcism more easily.

As to whether a possessed person should be exorcized privately or publicly in church—that is to say, with closed doors, or with the doors left open—it seems to me that there are as many different opinions on this subject as there are people to formulate them. Nevertheless, I do say this one thing: the Order of Exorcist is one of the seven sacred orders of the Holy Church, in which no works are done in a hidden or covert manner, but all quite openly and without secrecy.

Furthermore, Our Lord Jesus Christ Himself often cast demons out of possessed human beings in the presence of crowds of people, as the Gospels clearly show, such as in Matthew 17, Mark 9 and Luke 11. Through this, it may be concluded that the office of exorcist can, and perhaps ought, to be performed publicly, because of the many benefits that witnessing such things brings to the faithful. For a successful exorcism reveals to those who witness it the malice and wickedness of demons. It strengthens their faith, and it manifests to them the mercy and power of God. Seeing demons being cast out often causes those who witness it to repent of their own sins and to seek out holy remedies, and to lament sincerely their wrongdoings. Through such means, our blessed God reveals His own glory and promotes many useful effects among us, His faithful people—and these possible beneficial effects, as I see it, ought not to be impeded.

Nevertheless, it is not for us to give any rulings on this question. Rather, it is left to the judgment and discretion of Superiors, and the decisions of proper authorities is to be respected and followed in all particular cases.

Exorcism I

FOR PUTTING TO FLIGHT EVIL SPIRITS FROM THE BODIES OF
A POSSESSED PERSON

The priest who is to perform the exorcism should ensure that he is motivated by no light or spurious cause, but only by real necessity and charity to undertake this arduous task. He should firstly make sacramental confession, and fast for three days,[1] carefully cultivating humility of heart. Placing his trust in almighty God, he should enter a church together with the person who is afflicted by a demon. There they should genuflect before the Blessed Sacrament, or, if it is not present, at least before the altar.

Robed in his sacred vestments, attentively, firmly, and bravely, the exorcist should then make the sign of the cross on his forehead, on his lips and on his chest. As he does so, he says:

---

[1] This fasting for three days does not mean three days of complete abstinence from food, but rather a single meal (without meat) was permitted each day.

May the sign of the cross✝ be on my forehead. May the words of Christ✝ be on my lips. May the weapons✝ of Christ be in my heart.

Through the sign of the cross✝, liberate us from our foes, Lord our God.

O Power of the Father✝, strengthen me! O Wisdom of the Son✝, instruct me! O Love of the Holy Spirit✝, enlighten me!

Blessed be the day and the hour on which Our Lord Jesus Christ was born of the Virgin Mary.

In the name of the Father✝ and of the Son✝ and of the Holy Spirit✝. Amen.

May the Virgin Mary, with her merciful Son, bless us!

After this, the exorcist makes the sign of the cross upon the forehead, mouth, and chest of the possessed person. As he does so, he says:

O Power of the Father✝, comfort him! O Wisdom of the Son✝, instruct him! O Love of the Holy Spirit✝, enlighten him.

Blessed be the day and the hour on which Our Lord Jesus Christ was born of the Virgin Mary. In the name of the Father✝ and of the Son✝ and of the Holy Spirit✝. Amen.

The priest then says the Confiteor *("I confess to almighty God, and to you, my brethren, that I have greatly sinned...") and gives the absolution to the possessed person and to all present ("May Almighty God have mercy on us, forgive us our sins, and lead us to life everlasting.")*

After this, the exorcist imparts the following commands to any demons who may be on hand to assist or support with the principal demon who has possessed the person.

I command you, all you demons who have come to assist the demon who is vexing this creature of God, *N.*, on the part of the Holy Trinity—the Father✝, the Son✝ and the Holy Spirit✝. Under threat of immersion in the lake of fire and brimstone through the hands of your enemies; and under the threat of handing you into the power of your foes, and condemning you to suffer in the lake of fire and brimstone for a thousand years, I order that you give no assistance to the demon or demons who are vexing this creature of God, *N.*; but that you depart from here immediately, to the places assigned to you by almighty God.

Behold the cross✝ of the Lord! Flee from here, all forces of the adversary! The Lion of the tribe of Judah, the Root of David, has conquered.

The exorcist then imparts the following commands to the demons who are vexing the afflicted person.

I command you, O demons who vex this creature of God, *N.*, that, departing from him, you leave him free and well, without any harm to soul or body, so that he may be able to serve God his Creator.

And I direct all your adversaries, in the name of the Holy Trinity—the Father, the Son and the Holy Spirit, that they compel you to obey all my commands and precepts. And, by force of the same threats uttered before, I command that you say or do nothing which will disturb those here present or those absent, unless so commanded by me. In the name of the Father✝ and of the Son✝ and of the Holy Spirit✝. Amen.

After this, the exorcist places a stole around the neck of the possessed person, tying it with three knots. As he does so, he says:

O you abominable spirits and rebels against God! I command you, O spirits, I adjure, call, and constrain you, wherever you may be in this person, through the Father✝ and the Son✝ and the Holy Spirit✝, and through the most powerful name of God, Eloi, strong and wonderful. I exorcize and adjure you, O spirits, in virtue of the authority in which I function, through the strength of God, the most wise Creator, who created all things and who holds you within His dominion, that you understand and know the power of my words.

Knowing yourselves to be vanquished by these precepts, may you not dare to depart from this creature of God, who bears the image of Christ, without my permission. And thus I bind and enchain you, just as the saints of God did bind and constraint demons. And so, with this holy stole, I now bind you! In the name of the Father✝ and of the Son✝ and of the Holy Spirit✝. Amen.

The exorcists then places his hands upon the head of the possessed person, and says:

May all the power of the devil be extinguished in you, *N.*, through the imposition of our hands; or, rather, through the invocation of the holy archangels, angels, patriarchs, prophets, apostles, martyrs, confessors, virgins, and all the saints together. Amen.

After this, the following words are to be said, while making the sign of the cross on the forehead of the possessed person, whenever indicated in the text.

Ei✝, Eoloim✝, Eloa✝, Eheye✝, Tetragrammaton✝, Adonai✝, Shaddai✝, Sabaoth✝, Soter✝, Emanuel✝, Alpa and Omega✝, First and Last✝, Beginning and End✝, Hagios✝, Ischyros✝, Ho Theos✝, Athanatos✝, Agla✝, Jehovah✝, Homousion✝, Ja✝, Messiah✝, Efereheye✝, Christ conquers✝, Christ reigns✝, Christ commands✝, Uncreated Father✝, Uncreated Son✝, Uncreated Holy Spirit✝.

Through the sign of the cross, O God, free us from our enemies!

The exorcist then reads from the Gospel (John 1:1-14), with his hands placed upon the head of the possessed person throughout.

Then follows the response:
Praise to you, O Christ.

Next the exorcists adds:
Through the Gospel words that have been spoken, may all the power of the devil be extinguished in you, *N.*, and the power of God be poured forth into you. Amen.

Next, the Nicene Creed is said. Then follows:

Behold the cross✝ of the Lord! Flee from here, all forces of the adversary! The Lion of the tribe of Judah, the Root of David, has conquered.

John 16:24-30 is then read. The exorcist then says once more:

Behold the cross✝ of the Lord! Flee from here, all forces of the adversary! The Lion of the tribe of Judah, the Root of David, has conquered.

After this, Psalm 50 ('Miserere mei, Deus') *is said. Then follows again the verse:*

Behold the cross✝ of the Lord! Flee from here, all forces of the adversary! The Lion of the tribe of Judah, the Root of David, has conquered.

After this, Psalm 69 ('Deus in adjutorium meum intende...') *is said, concluding with a 'Glory be...'.*
Then the exorcist continues:

Lord, do not recall our guilt nor that of our parents, and do not repay us according to our sins.

Then, genuflecting, the following litany is prayed.

Lord have mercy. Christ have mercy. Lord have mercy
Christ, hear us. Christ, graciously hear us.
God the Father in Heaven, have mercy on us.
God the Son, Redeemer of the world, have mercy on us.
God the Holy Spirit, have mercy on us.
Holy Trinity, one God, have mercy on us.
Holy Mary, pray for us.
Holy Mother of God, pray for us.
Holy Virgin of virgins, pray for us.
St. Michael, pray for us.

St. Gabriel, pray for us.
St. Raphael, pray for us.
All holy Angels and Archangels, pray for us.
All holy orders of the Blessed Spirits, pray for us.
St. John the Baptist, pray for us.
St. Joseph, pray for us.
All holy Prophets and Patriarchs, pray for us.
St. Peter, pray for us.

[Editor's note: Here follows a lengthy list of saints, each followed by 'Pray for us.' The saint names are given in order below, each of which is to be followed by 'Pray for us.']

St. Paul, St. Andrew, St. James, St. John, St. Thomas, St. Philipp, St. James, St. Bartholomew, St. Matthew, St. Simon, St. Thaddeus, St. Matthias, St. Barnabas, St. Luke, St. Mark, All holy Apostles and Evangelists, All holy disciples of the Lord, All Holy Innocents, St. Stephen, St. Laurence, St. Vincent, St. Cyprian, St. Fabian and St. Sebastian, St. John and St. Paul, St. Cosmas and St. Damian, St. Gervaisius and St. Protasius, All holy Martyrs, St. Sylvester, St. Gregory, St. Ambrose, St. Augustine, St. Geminianus, St. Jerome, St. Martin, St. Nicolaus, St. Louis, St. Bonaventure, All holy Bishops and Confessors, All holy Doctors, St. Benedict, St. Francis, St. Dominic, St. Anthony, St. Bernadine, St. Bernard, All holy Priests, All holy monks and hermits, St. Anne, St. Mary Magdalene, St. Agnes, St. Lucy, St. Cecilia, St. Agatha, St. Catherine, St. Clare, St. Elisabeth, St. Anastasia, All holy Virgins and widows.

All saints of God, intercede for him.

Be merciful, spare him, O Lord.

From all evil: free him, O Lord.
From all sin: free him, O Lord.

From Your wrath: free him, O Lord.
From sudden and unexpected death: free him, O Lord.
From the snares of the devil: free him, O Lord.
From anger, hatred, and all evil will: free him, O Lord.
From the spirit of fornication: free him, O Lord.
From lightning and tempest: free him, O Lord.
From everlasting death: free him, O Lord.

Through the mystery of Your holy Incarnation: free him, O Lord.
Through Your Advent: free him, O Lord.
Through Your Nativity: free him, O Lord.
Through Your baptism and sacred fasting: free him, O Lord.
Through Your cross and passion: free him, O Lord.
Through Your death and burial: free him, O Lord.
Through Your holy Resurrection: free him, O Lord.
Through Your glorious Ascension: free him, O Lord.
Through the coming of the Holy Spirit, the Paraclete: free him, O Lord.
On the Day of Judgment: free him, O Lord.

We sinners implore You:
That You give to him peace, we implore You.
That Your mercy and kindness may guard him, we implore You.
That You deign to turn Your eyes of mercy towards him, we implore You.
That You protect him from tribulation and vexation and deign to relieve him, we implore You.
That You deign to bless and liberate this Your servant, N., we implore You.
That this Your servant, N., You deign to rescue from the vexation of the devil, we implore You.
That You deign to liberate this Your servant, N., from the infestation of demons, we implore You.

That You deign to hear us, we implore You.
Son of God, we implore You.

Lamb of God who take away the sins of the world; spare him, O Lord.
Lamb of God, who take away the sins of the world; graciously hear us, O Lord.
Lamb of God, who take away the sins of the world; have mercy on us.

Then the exorcist addresses the demon thus:
Behold the cross✝ of the Lord! Flee from here, all forces of the adversary! The Lion of the tribe of Judah, the Root of David, has conquered.

Next follows the prayer:
Lord Jesus Christ, for the redemption of the world You willed to be persecuted by the Jews; to be betrayed by Judas with a kiss; to be bound in chains by the hands of sinners; to be led away as a meek lamb to the sacrifice; to be accused unjustly before Pilate; to be pierced with sharp nails; to be afflicted with scourging and other torments; to be crowned with thorns; to be struck with blows; to be raised up on the cross among criminals; to be given vinegar and gall to drink; and to be wounded with a lance.

Lord Jesus Christ, through these most holy sufferings of Yours, which I, a miserable and unworthy sinner, call to mind, and through Your holy cross, I pray that You do not regard my sins, and the sins of this Your creature, *N.*; but, through Your great mercy, to free him from the vexations of the devil; who live and reign forever and ever. Amen.

Then the exorcist addresses the demon thus:

Behold the cross✝ of the Lord! Flee from here, all forces of the adversary! The Lion of the tribe of Judah, the Root of David, has conquered.

The exorcist then continues:

O good cross, O worthy cross, wood above all woods! Through this sign of the cross✝, may all evil be repelled. May all phantasms depart from hence, harming the mind of no-one.

Then the exorcist addresses the demon thus:

Behold the cross✝ of the Lord! Flee from here, all forces of the adversary! The Lion of the tribe of Judah, the Root of David, has conquered.

The prayer continues:

Lord, graciously hear me prayer, and let my cries come before You. Let Your ears receive the voice of my supplication. O Lord, be unto me a tower of strength, in the face of all evil spirits. Lay these upon a rack of torment, and disperse them as chaff before the wind!

Next follows the prayer:

Lord, God almighty, Author of invincible strength and King of an unconquerable empire, magnificent Victor, You crush the forces of all adversaries and combat all hostile powers. You created all things out of nothing by Your word alone, and You expelled Lucifer and all his followers as rebels from the highest Heaven. Through Your Son, You reconciled the highest with the lowest. You desire not the death of the sinner nor do You rejoice to see the dying perish; rather it is Yours to have mercy and to spare.

Have mercy on Your creature, *N.*, not viewing him in accordance with his sins but rather according to Your great mercy. Free him from all the snares of evil spirits, in whatever manner he may be bound, and liberate him from all infestation and affliction of those spirits by which he is afflicted. Do this, O Lord, as once You freed Mary Magdalene from seven unclean spirits, and the daughter of the woman of Canaan from the vexation of demons. Even thus, now deign to free *N.* from all the evil spirits afflicting him. Do this, O Lord, as once You freed Jonah from the whale; and Susanna from those who accused her falsely; and David from the evil sword and the hands of Saul; and the three young men from the fiery furnace; and Daniel from the den of lions; and Isaac from the hands of his father; and Joseph from the prison of Pharoah. Even thus, now deign to free this Your creature, *N.*, who has been redeemed by the Blood of Your Son and reborn in baptism, from all vexation of evil spirits and demons.

You gave to Your apostles authority over evil spirits and their powers, and the ability to dispel them from human bodies, and the ability to cure the ill. Even thus, deign to grant unto me, Your unworthy servant, reborn in the waters of baptism and ordained for the service of Your most holy name, the power of Your grace to put to flight all evil spirits from this Your creature, *N.*, by the invocation of Your most holy name. Through Our Lord Jesus Christ. Amen.

Then the exorcist addresses the demon thus:
Behold the cross✝ of the Lord! Flee from here, all forces of the adversary! The Lion of the tribe of Judah, the Root of David, has conquered.

Next follows the prayer:
Almighty and eternal God, Father of Our Lord Jesus Christ, we humbly implore You that You command these spirits who have taken possession of Your servant, *N.*, that they recede from him. Free him, we pray, for he believes in the true Liberator, Our Lord Jesus Christ, who lives and reign with You in the unity of the Holy Spirit, God forever and ever. Amen.

Then the exorcist addresses the demon thus:
Behold the cross✝ of the Lord! Flee from here, all forces of the adversary! The Lion of the tribe of Judah, the Root of David, has conquered.

Here the exorcist arises. Before he commences to command the demons, he is to exorcize the possessed person as follows:
I exorcize you, *N.*, in the name of God the almighty Father✝, in the name His Son Our Lord Jesus Christ✝, in the power of the Holy Spirit✝, so that you may become a clean, holy vessel, purged from all stain of iniquity.

All works of witchcraft, spells, and any other works of sorcery upon your body or around it, I, *N.*, a sinner and an unworthy servant of God, by the authority granted to me, in the name of the same God the almighty Father, in the name of His Son, Our Lord Jesus Christ, and in the power of the Holy Spirit, hereby dissolve and make to be null.

Then, addressing the demon(s), he says:
I command you, O accursed devil and your associates, that you shall no longer have the power of remaining in this body, from the soles of his feet to the top of his head. Rather, you must immediately depart from it, taking with you all your works of witchcraft and spells. I command this

through Him who is to come to judge, through fire, the living and the dead and the world. Amen.

Next follows the prayer:
God of mercy, merciful God, according to the multitude of Your mercies, You correct those whom You love, and You move to emendation those whom You accept. We invoke You, Lord, that You deign to confer grace upon your servant, *N.*, who suffers torments in body and spirit. We implore that whatever in him has been corrupted by earthly fragility and whatever in him has been corrupted by diabolic fraud, You may join to the unity of the body of the Church, the instrument of redemption.

O Lord, have mercy on his mourning, have mercy on his tears! As he has no confidence in anything except Your mercy, admit him to the sacrament of reconciliation with You. Amen.

At this point, the possessed person is to be sprinkled with holy water. Then the following exorcism is said over him.

I exorcize you, *N.*, who have been reborn in the waters of sacred baptism, through the living God✝, through the true God✝, through the holy God✝, through God who redeemed you by His precious blood. May you become a person liberated from demonic influence, and may all phantoms and frauds of the devil be put to flight from you, and all unclean spirits expelled; through Him who is to come to judge the living and the dead, Our Lord Jesus Christ. Amen.

Then the following prayer is said:
O God, who rule all Your actions with merciful love, incline Your ear to our pleading. Kindly look upon and visit Your

servant, *N.*, who is laboring against his affliction, and present to him the medicine of Your heavenly grace and healing. Amen.

Here the possessed person is sprinkled with holy water again. With great faith and hope, the exorcist then addressed the demon(s) dwelling within the body of the afflicted person, saying:
Hear, O devil and unclean spirit! I admonish you and exorcize you✝. I command you, O tempter—who are vain, insensate, false, heretical, vacuous, inimical, drunk, scornful, foolish, and cut off from the grace of God and Christ.

I exorcize you through Him✝ who for our sake descended to the earth, and was announced by the angel, made flesh through the Holy Spirit, born of the Virgin Mary, increased in age and wisdom, and at the age of twelve years entered the temple and, sitting amongst the learned men, wisely questioned them.

I adjure you through Him✝ who was baptized by John the Baptist in the River Jordan, who was tempted by the devil, and betrayed by His disciple Judas, arrested, mocked, scourged, given vinegar and gall to drink, chained, crowned with thorns, stripped naked, and over whose garment lots were cast.

I command you through Him✝ who was crucified, died and was buried, and on the third day rose from the dead, ascended into Heaven, and is seated at the right hand of God the Father, and who is to come again to judge the living and the dead through fire.

I command that you to depart immediately from this vessel, this creation of God, and attack neither myself or anyone else here present, and cause no harm to him.

I exorcize you through Him✝ whom the angel Gabriel announced was to be born of the womb of the Virgin Mary, and whom John the Baptist saluted while in the womb of Elizabeth. I command you that whatever I ask you, you shall answer, and speak to me the truth regarding who is your master, and by what name you are known, whether or not you are within this person's body, and whether you are alone or accompanied by a legion of others, or many legions of others.

Here the exorcist questions the demon, on the following matters:
- *what is its name*
- *how many associates it has*
- *who is its master*
- *under what demonic powers it is working*
- *what is the reason for it attacking this particular person*
- *if it is working as a result of a spell or other work of witchcraft, and, if so, how such a spell is able to be dissolved*
- *how long it has been vexing this person*
- *which saint it fears most strongly*
- *whom it regards as its greatest or particular foes, both among the angels and saints in Heaven and the demons in hell*
- *what sign it will give upon departing from the person of whom it has taken possession.*

Next the exorcist should command the demon that it is not to harm the afflicted person when it departs from them, and that it is never to return to them again.

The exorcist should be prudent and circumspect in his questioning, lest he be deceived by the demon whom he is interrogating. He should carefully retain humility in his mind, which is necessary to liberate a creature of God from possession and to question a demon with safety.

If the demon refuses to respond to the questions or to depart at this point, the exorcist is to proceed to the following adjuration.

I adjure you, therefore, you murderer, reprobate, and son of perdition, through Him✝ whose sign appeared in the Heavens and was seen by the shepherd, whom the Magi adored and whom angels and archangels praise, that immediately you go out from this vessel and creation of Christ; and then you should go into the depths of the sea, or into a fruitless tree, or into a deserted place which no Christians inhabit and no person approaches. There, may fire from Heaven burn you! May the majesty of God the Holy Trinity—the Father✝, the Son✝, and the Holy Spirit✝—compel you immediately to depart.

I adjure you, O iniquitous demon, through Him✝ whose name is Jesus of Nazareth, that, having heard the word of the Lord, you leave this servant of God. I adjure you through Him whose birth the holy angels acclaimed, singing: "Glory to God in the highest!" I adjure you through Him whom the Magi, coming from the east, adored, offering gold, frankincense, and myrrh, as had been foretold. I adjure you through Him✝ at whose birth a star appeared in the Heavens, which the prophet Balaam had predicted, saying: "A star will be born out of Jacob;"[2] and through Him whom the mute animals recognized, as is written: "The ox knows its Master, as does the donkey within the stable of its Lord."[3]

---

[2] Number 24:17.
[3] Isaiah 1:3.

I adjure you through Him✝ whom Herod wished to kill but was not able, and for whom the Holy Innocents were slaughtered, and by whose Blood the celestial Jerusalem is adorned. I adjure you through Him✝ who with His mother fled into Egypt, and who converted water into wine in Galilee, and whom Pilate crowned with a crown of thorns and crucified, and whose side Longinus opened with a lance, and who on the cross cried out: "*Eli, Eli, lema sabachthani.*"

I adjure you through Him✝ who was found in the temple in the midst of the Doctors of the Law, and who was raised up on the cross into mid-air amidst thieves, and who, after the Resurrection, stood in the midst of His disciples, saying: "Peace be with you! Do not fear."

I adjure you through Him✝ who died, was buried, and who descended into the underworld and there took those who were His own from the devil, and liberated the first man Adam; and who on the third day rose from the dead, and after forty days ascended into Heaven.

May He Himself expel you from this body and the limbs of this creature of God, *N.* May He who once cast you out of Heaven compel you to reveal to me the name of your master, and whether you are alone here or have a legion of your fellow demons accompanying you.

I adjure you through Him✝ who created Paradise from which flow the four rivers—Geon, Phison, Tigris, and Euphrates—and whom you once tried to tempt, saying: "If You are the Son of God, turn these stones into bread," and again: "If You are the Son of God, cast Yourself down from here," and again: "All this I will give to You, if You fall down and worship me." I adjure you through Him✝ who once said to you: "Depart from here, Satan, you shall not put the Lord your God to the test, but Him alone shall you worship and serve!"

Here the exorcist continues with his adjuration of the demon:

O wicked demon and ancient serpent, I adjure you through the most holy name of God✝, great and most strong, which all the tongues of the living are not sufficient to express, nor the mind or the senses to comprehend, which is the Tetragrammaton.

I adjure you through the name of God✝, Alpha and Omega; Jesus, our Redemption; the Life and the Resurrection: our salvation and defense and the remission of our sins. I adjure you through the name of God, Adonai, which is great and marvelous, ineffable Creator, and wondrous Son of God, indescribable and invisible Spirit; inextinguishable Splendor; inseparable Three and indivisible One. Through these holy names I command you, O demon, that you immediately leave this body, without any harm or terror to this creature of God or any ill to any other person, and that you leave no trace of yourself here!

I adjure you, O demon, through the Father✝, the Son✝, and the Holy Spirit✝, and through that spiritual anointing of Him who is the Triune God.

Again, I adjure you through her✝ who nursed Christ and carried in her womb the God who created her. I command that you no longer have power to remain in the creature of God, *N.*

I adjure you through St. Michael the Archangel✝, who cast you from Heaven by the strength of God when he fought with the dragon and overcame him. I command that you leave the place where you now are, and depart to some deserted place or to the depths of the abyss where you shall be able to hurt no-one.

I adjure you through St. Gabriel the Archangel✝, who announced the coming and Incarnation of Our Lord Jesus Christ to the Blessed Virgin Mary, when he said: "Hail Mary, full of grace, the Lord is with thee; blessed art thou among women." I command that, upon hearing these words, you promptly depart from this creature of God, N., without causing terror to anyone.

I adjure you, O demon, through St. Raphael✝, who guarded Tobias and Sarah and liberated them from a demon, and who, through the strength of God, bound the demon Asmodeus so that he was by no means able to harm them. I command you to depart immediately from this creature of God, N., never to return, and that you will retain no power to harm him.

I adjure you, O demon, through all the holy Angels, Archangels, Thrones, Dominions, Principalities, Powers, Virtues, Cherubim and Seraphim✝, who never cease to proclaim with one voice, singing: "Holy, holy, holy Lord God Sabaoth."

Here the exorcist continues with his adjuration of the demon:

Again I adjure you, O accursed demon✝, through all the prayers of the patriarchs and the merits of the prophets and the sufferings of the apostles and the victories of the martyrs, and through the faith of the holy confessors and the prayers of the virgins, and through the intercession of all the saints of God who have pleased God since the beginning of the world, that you should immediately recede and depart from this creature of God, *N.* .

Again I adjure you, O demon✝, through holy Abel, who was the first among the martyrs, through holy Enoch, who walked in the presence of God and was taken up out of the world, and through holy Noah, who was saved in the flood because of his righteousness. I adjure you through the faith of Abraham, who believed in God and whose faith was reputed to him as righteousness; and through holy Isaac, who was obedient to his father even unto death, and who pre-figured Our Lord Jesus Christ offered up for our salvation; and through blessed Jacob, who saw the angel of the Lord coming to his aid.

Again I adjure you, O demon✝, through holy Moses, to whom the Lord spoke face to face; and through the holy prophets, Amos, Micah, Hosea, Joel, Obadiah, Habakkuk, Jonah, Zephaniah, Haggai, Zachariah, Malachi, Esdras, Jeremiah, Isaiah, Ezekiel, David; and through all other holy prophets✝, I adjure you, that in whatever matter I question you, you speak to me the pure truth without delay, and that in whatever I command you, you do not refuse or resist.

I adjure you through St. John the Baptist, greater than whom was none among the men born of women. I adjure you through the twelve Apostles of Our Lord Jesus Christ✝, and through all His holy disciples, and through St. Peter, the Prince of the Apostles, that you should immediately depart from this creature of God, *N.*, leaving all his members unharmed, just as you found them when first you entered him. I command that whatever I ask you about, you immediately respond with the whole truth, and that you manifest to me whatever I ask of you.

Through the merits of all the saints of God, I order that you depart immediately from this servant of God at my command, carrying to him no pain or injury, nor pain and injury to any other person; and that you depart then to the depth of the abyss, never to come forth until the Day of Judgment. Amen.

Behold the cross✝ of the Lord! Flee from here, all forces of the adversary! The Lion of the tribe of Judah, the Root of David, has conquered.

Here the exorcist should question the demon about its exit (whether it has left already, or what sign it will give of its departure). Next, he continues in the following fashion:

I adjure you✝, O ancient serpent, through the Judge of the living and the dead, through the Creator of the world, through Him who has the power to cast you into Gehenna, that you immediately depart from this servant of God, *N.*, who has fled to the protection of His holy Church.

I adjure you✝ not through my own feebleness, but through the strength of the Holy Spirit, that you depart from this servant of God, *N.*, whom Our Lord Jesus Christ made in His own image and likeness.

Begone, begone! — not in obedience to me personally, but in obedience to me as a minister of Christ. May the power of Him✝, who, when affixed to the cross, has placed you under His command, compel you.

Fear the arm of Him who led the souls of the just from the torments of hell. May this human body be a source of terror to you, and may the image of God within it be terror to you. Do not refuse nor delay to depart from this person, for it is

God's will that He Himself should dwell within each human being. And, although you know well that I am a sinner, do not imagine that I am to be treated with contempt or disdain by you.

God✝ commands you.

The majesty of Christ✝ commands you.

God the Father✝ commands you.

The Son✝ commands you.

The Holy Spirit✝ commands you.
The faith of the apostles Peter and Paul and all the other apostles✝ commands you.

The blood of the martyrs✝ commands you.

The sacrament of the cross✝ commands you.

The mystery and virtue of the cross✝ commands you.

Jesus of Nazareth✝ commands you.

The Word made flesh✝ commands you.

Depart from here, O transgressor, seducer, full of all deceit and falsehood, enemy of the truth! Most stubborn and impious one, yield your place to Christ, in whom nothing is to be found of your evil works, and who has despoiled you and destroyed your kingdom, who has bound you as a sacrifice, and broken your vessel, and who has cast you into the outer darkness prepared for you and your ministers.

Why do you so truculently resist? Why do you so audaciously refuse?

You are guilty in the sight of God almighty, whose statutes you have transgressed.
You are guilty in the sight of Jesus Christ His Son, whom you boldly tried to tempt, and conspired to crucify.

You are guilty in the sight of the human race, whom you tricked into eating the fruit of death by means of your persuasions.

And so I adjure you✝, O most wicked dragon, in the name of the immaculate Lamb—who walked among asps and vipers, and who trampled on the lion and dragon—that you depart from this man, that you depart from this Church of God;[4] that you tremble and flee at the invocation of name of Him before whom hell fears, and to whom the Virtues and Powers of Heaven are subject, and whom Cherubim and Seraphim with one voice unceasingly praise, saying, "Holy, holy, holy Lord God Sabaoth."

Jesus of Nazareth commands you, He who once commanded you to depart from a possessed man, and without whose permission you did not presume to enter even the herd of swine. In His name✝, depart now from this man whom He created.

It is hard for you to resist the will of Christ, it is hard for you to kick against the goad, for the longer you take to leave, the harsher shall be the punishment which awaits you. For you are not defying merely a human being now, but Him who is the Lord of the living and the dead, and who is to come to judge the living and the dead and the world with fire. Amen.

The exorcist then continues:

Again and again, I adjure you✝, O demon, through Him who gave power to His disciples to give sight to the blind, to cleanse lepers, to raise the dead, and to cure all afflictions. I adjure you through Him who restored the first man,

---

[4] It is assumed that this exorcism is taking place in a church or chapel. See Chapter XV.

Adam, through the wood of the holy cross, and who opened the eyes of the man born blind, and who raised up the dead Lazarus from the tomb after four days, and who cured all illness by His own strength, and who annulled the magical illusions of the sorcerers Jannes and Mambres.[5]

And through this exorcism, and through all other adjurations, and through all holy words and offices which are celebrated throughout the entire whole world—through all these, I command you, wherever you may be and whoever you may be, that immediately you depart, like smoke that is blown away, and go forth to some deserted place or to the depths of the abyss, never again to return and never again to inflict harm on anyone.

In the name of the Father✝, the Son✝, and the Holy Spirit✝. Amen.

---

[5] According to tradition, these were the Egyptian magicians who contended with Moses in Exodus 7.

Exorcism II

In the name of the Father✝, and of the Son✝, and of the Holy Spirit✝. Amen.

May God arise and disperse His enemies, and put to flight from His face all those who hate Him. As smoke that is blown away, so may they be blown away; as wax that melts before the presence of the fire, so may all demons be defeated before our presence.

Here the exorcist shows the cross to the person possessed, and says:

Behold the cross✝ of Our Lord Jesus Christ! Flee from here, all you adversaries of Christ, for He so wills it. Uncreated Father✝, uncreated Son✝, and uncreated Holy Spirit✝, the Lion of the tribe of Judah, the Root of David, has conquered and is victorious.

Hail, holy cross, through which such victories have been given! Make me do Your will, and put to flight all those who would do us harm. Grant unto me virtue, mercy, peace, and salvation. Be my hope while I am living and my protection if I should die.

Behold the cross✝ of Our Lord Jesus Christ! Flee from here, all you adversaries of Him, for Christ so wills it. Through this sign of the cross, God will dispel all forces of evil. They shall do no harm to the mind or soul, and all phantasms will recede from hence.

O good cross, O worthy cross, O wood above all woods! The cross is the way of virtue; the cross is the way of true salvation. The cross is the strength of humanity. The cross raises us up to the Lord!

Here the exorcist kneels, saying:

Almighty Lord, Creator of Heaven and earth, Jesus Christ, King of kings, highest power, ruling all justly and in holy order, coming from the Heavens and born of the holy Virgin! The hand of all-powerful Heaven has been extended to the earth through You, and You have afterwards bestowed holy miracles in a thousand ways. Affixed to the cross, by Your blood you have saved the world, and hence You have granted to Your servants a powerful emblem of victory, by means of which they are able to constrain all the frauds and malice of demons.

I implore You, O Christ, lover of the human race, that You expel all the wicked works of this demon, and by Your holy words annul all its evil deeds, and by Your wounds expel all its foul venom.

When the faithful people witness this, they shall praise You forever, for ages unending, and proclaim You as Creator of all the Heavens and the earth, who, with the Father and the Holy Spirit, live and reign forever and ever. Amen.

Here the exorcist arises and, addressing the demon, says:

O you most wicked demon, and great deceiver of souls! You promise splendid things out of these evils as if you were a god; but this shall be your end, and you shall be addressed as 'Master' no more. For you are deceived, and you will come to be scorned everywhere.

I command you✝, O demon, through the living God, in the strength of the Holy Spirit; and through Him who created You and cast You out of Heaven, and through the dreadful Day of Judgment; and through the ineffable name of the Lord—that you tell me who you are and how you are to be addressed.

And through these holy names of God, you shall depart without delay from this creature of God, *N.*, at my command, carrying no pain to them, nor hurt to anyone, immediately, and without harm to any person whatsoever. El✝, Elohim✝, Adonai✝, Shaddai✝, Soter✝, Emmanuel✝, Tetragrammaton✝, Alpha✝ and Omega✝, Beginning and End✝, Hagios✝, Ischyros✝, Ho Theos✝, Athanatos✝, Agla✝, Ieshoua✝, Homousion✝, Ya✝, Jesus✝, Christ✝, Messiah✝, Eloa✝, Eheye✝.

Again, I command you, O demon, through the living God✝, through the true God✝, through the holy God✝, through the Father✝, through the Son✝, and through the Holy Spirit✝, through the Blessed Virgin Mary, through the whole celestial court, and through all others, by which you are able to be compelled and constrained, that you manifest yourself immediately, O wicked spirit, and give a true answer to whatsoever I shall ask of you!

Here the exorcist is able to question the demon possessing the body, binding it to speak truly in all matters which pertain to the liberation of the possessed person.

After this, the following Gospel passages are read. [At the end of each passage, the response "Praise to You, O Christ," is said.]

John 1:1-14.
Mark 16:14-20.
Luke 11:14-28.
Matthew 4:1-11.
Luke 13:6-17.
Luke 4:38-44.
Mark 9:16-28.

The exorcist then says the following exorcism:

I exorcize you, O unclean spirit, you tempter and devil—enemy, lustful, insipid, and cast out from the grace of God and Christ! I exorcize and adjure you through Him who for our sake descended to the earth and was incarnate of the Holy Spirit and was born of the Virgin Mary; I adjure you that, immediately and without delay, you come out and flee from this vessel and creation of God, without harm to this person, *N.*, nor to any other person.

I exorcize you, through Him whom the angel Gabriel announced in the womb of the Virgin Mary. I exorcize you, through Him whom, while still in the womb of the Virgin Mary, John the Baptist saluted out of Elizabeth.

Through Him I adjure and constrain you, that—if you are in this body—you speak to me and indicate to me the name of yourself or your master.

I command you, O deceived one, you murderer and son of perdition—through Him whose sign appeared in the Heaven which the shepherds saw, whom the Magi adored, whom the angels and archangels praise together. He Himself will cast you out of this vessel, this image of God, and will send you into the depths of the sea or a deserted place inhabited by no human being, where the Holy Trinity—the Father, the Son, and the Holy Spirit—will burn you with fire from Heaven!

I adjure you through Him whose name is Jesus the Nazarene; whom King Herod wished to kill but was not able to do so, and for whose sake were killed the Holy Innocents, by whose blood the Holy Jerusalem in Heaven is adorned.

I command, exorcize, and constrain you, through Him who with His mother fled into Egypt. I adjure you by the crown of Christ. I exorcize and adjure you through Him who transformed water into wine in Cana in Galilee; whom Pilate crucified; whom Longinus pierced with a lance; and who cried out on the cross, "*Eli, Eli, lema sabachthani*"; and who descended to the inferno and freed His own who were held captive there by the devil; by Him who on the third day rose again, and after forty days ascended into Heaven; and who thereby liberated the first Adam from captivity.

May He Himself expel you, you heretical and false murderer, who are separated from Jesus Christ and from the cross of Christ!

I exorcize and adjure you through Him who made the four rivers—Geon, Phison, Tigris and Euphrates—to flow forth from Paradise, so that you will not have the authority or power to withhold your name from me, but will immediately tell me who you are and who is your master; for I am the servant and minister of Christ.

Here the exorcist asks the name of the demon and his associates, and why he [or they] have taken possession of the person, and about all other matters pertaining to the liberation of the person possessed.

The exorcist then continues thus:

Listen, therefore, most malign demon; listen, O damned and reprobate creature, cursed by God; listen, I say, O proud one!

You abandoned the God who created you, and were forgetful of your Lord and Creator, who cast you, together with your leader, Satan, and the other demons who followed him, into the eternal fire, all because of your pride.

I place my confidence in the virtue and power of this God and Creator, and not in my own merits, O accursed devil, most impure Satan, and most proud spirit! Because of the perversity of your decision, you chose to contradict God, and did not wish to follow His ordinances, nor did you wish to be converted to Him. You did this by disdaining and relinquishing the domicile of the almighty God—who has existed as Three and One before the world began, and who is the cause of all existing creatures, such that if He withdraws His power and rule, they would all cease to exist in a single blink of the eye. You wished neither to obey Him faithfully, as all the blessed spirits had done who enjoy the fullness of happiness.

Rather you took delight in the perverse order of pride and envy—you and all the blinded angels who followed your strength. And because of this impure choice of yours, you were cast down from the heights of Heaven and drawn into the nether darkness. And on the Day of Judgment you are destined to be cast into the infernal abyss of hell, where you shall be tortured day and night, and the fumes of your torments shall ascend forever and ever!

I exorcize and anathemize you, whether you are one or many, and command that you declare to me now how it was that you presumed to enter into this servant of God, N., signed and initiated as he is with the divine mysteries— whether through food or drink, or in whatever superstitious act of witchcraft, or through whatever enchantment made against this servant of God.

And all such acts of witchcraft or enchantment I hereby annul and declare to be void, through the singular power and virtue of the invincible King and Lord of all, our Savior Jesus Christ, who came into this world to dissolve and cancel all the works of Satan. And just as He, through our fathers St. Peter and St. Paul, once annulled all the spells and enchantment of your servant, Simon Magus; and just as He, through the apostle St. Bartholomew once healed all those who had been wounded by the demon inhabiting the idol Astaroth; and just as He, through the holy prophet Moses, once overcame the illusions of the Egyptian magicians, Jannes and Mambres through the finger of God almighty; so now, through the finger of the same omnipotent God—that is, the Holy Spirit, who proceeds from the Father and the Son—even so we now hereby render naught all the sorcerous arts and illusions cast over this His servant, *N.* Let this be so, whether such acts of witchcraft and enchantment were performed through the malice of your envy, with which you, O wicked and impure spirit, lay snares against human salvation, according to your evil will; or whether this occurred through the just dispensation of our almighty Lord and God; or whether it is the result of the sins of this person whom you have afflicted, or those of his parents. Against all of these, I place the plenitude of redemption of the most precious Blood of Our Lord Jesus Christ, who loved us, and washed us from our sins in His own Blood.

Coming into this world, He conquered your prince, not only by His power, but also at the price of His own most precious Blood. The proud one He bound, breaking his vessel and despoiling his dominions and powers; and, righteously and powerfully, He rescued us from your reign. And our blessed God and Lord, ascending into Heaven as our Head, gave power to His disciples and to His faithful of expelling you from human bodies, when He said: "In My name, they shall cast out demons." And in another place, He said to His apostles and disciples: "I have given you virtue and power over all demons and strength of the enemy." And He willed ourselves, though we are unworthy, to be among the number of those to whom this power was given. For in our priestly ministry, at the table of the altar, He transubstantiates the substance of bread and wine into His own Body and Blood. By virtue of this, and in the power given to me by our almighty God and Lord Jesus Christ, I command you, O unclean spirit—whether you are one or many, and however you audaciously presumed to enter into this servant of God, *N.*, who is initiated by the divine sacraments (whether it was through food or drink, or by any work or deception of witchcraft cast upon this servant of God, *N.*) I command you in the name of God the almighty Father✝, His Son Our Lord Jesus Christ✝, and the

Holy Spirit✝, that you depart from this servant of God, *N.*, without any harm to him. You shall no longer presume to enter into him, nor remain in him for a moment, nor perturb his interior or exterior senses, from the soles of his feet to the top of his head. Nor shall you agitate his feelings, nor generate any deficiencies in him, nor vex him with any weakness, nor perturb his tranquility either in the hours of the day or of the night.

And if you impertinently disdain to obey my commands—or rather those of the true God, Our Lord Jesus Christ, the highest and invincible King—may this same God and Lord Jesus Christ (through the virtues of His most sacred passion and through the merits of the Blessed Virgin Mary, and the merits of all the holy angels, the patriarchs, prophets, apostles, martyrs, confessors, and virgins) send His angel against you, as once He did against the contemptuous and hard-hearted Pharaoh. For it was He who cast you and your apostate associates into the lake of fire and brimstone, where you will be tormented day and night, and the smoke of your torments shall arise forever and ever. Amen.

Therefore, O accursed demon, you creature damned and condemned by God forever for your wickedness, O unclean spirit, wherever you hide in the body of this person, *N.*, recognize the judgment that has been passed upon you, and know the most just sentence of your damnation!

And even though it is against your most wicked will and under compulsion, give honor to the true and living God✝, and to Jesus Christ our Lord and Savior✝, give honor to the Holy Spirit the Paraclete✝, and depart forthwith from this servant of God, *N.*, and never again approach him, for Our Lord Jesus Christ has deigned to call him to Himself, through His gift of His grace and through the font of sacred baptism. And you, O devil accursed and damned and deserving of damnation, unclean spirit, never again dare to violate this sign of the holy cross, through the name and virtue of the same Jesus Christ Our Lord, who is to come to judge the living and the dead and the world through fire. Amen.

Here the exorcist places his hands upon the head of the afflicted person, and says this prayer:

O Lord, expel the devil from this Your creature, *N.*, from his head, from his hairs, from the top of his head, from his forehead, from his eyes, from his tongue, from beneath his tongue, from his nostrils, from his neck, from his cheeks, from his teeth, from his throat, from his gums, from his mouth, from his palate, from his skull, from the membranes of his skull, from his eyelashes, from his eyebrows, from his skin, from his feet, from his shins, from his knees, from his calves, from his private parts, from his kidneys, from his sides, from his upper and lower intestines, from his thighs, from his gut, from his stomach, from his heart, from his shoulder blades, from his shoulders, from his chest, from his breast, from his arms, from his hands, from his nails, from his bones, from his nerves, from his veins, from the marrow of his bones, from his lungs, from all the joints of his limbs, and from his whole body, both inside and outside, and from the five senses of his body and soul, so that it shall have no place whatsoever within him.

Let this person be healed and saved through the invocation of the most holy name of Your only-begotten Son✝, and through the invocation of the co-eternal Holy Spirit✝. Almighty God, who deigned to create the body and soul of this your creature, *N.*, may You now deign to heal and make well his whole body and soul. Through the same Jesus

Christ✝, Your Son, Our Lord, who lives and reigns with You in the unity of the Holy Spirit✝, God✝ forever and ever. Amen.

Editor's note

The following chapters are taken from the book The Cudgel of Demons (Fustis Daemonum) *by Fr. Girolamo Menghi. It was written as a kind of supplement to* The Scourge of Demons. *In Chapter XIV of* The Scourge of Demons *(see above), Menghi refers the reader to the chapters given here. This reference was clearly a subsequent interpolation to the original, as* The Cudgel of Demons *was, in fact, a later work (first appearing in 1584, some eight years after the original publication of* The Scourge of Demons*). For the sake of completeness, these extremely important chapters (which contain information on the indications of demonic possession and affliction by witchcraft) are included in full below.*

Appendix: The Cudgel of Demons

Chapter XI: The Causes and Ways in Which Demons Enter Human Bodies, and the Signs and Effects by Which a Possessed Person Can Be Known

A S WE HAVE often stated, demons have a thousand ways and methods of harming the human race. Although all persons should be aware of these, as a way of avoiding sin and temptation and the various snares of demons, nevertheless exorcists should know the ways in which demons attack bodies and souls more particularly, and how it may be determined if they are vexing a particular person or not. The exorcist ought to know also all matters pertaining to commanding and adjuring demons, so that, with the help of God, he is able to liberate their victims from their atrocious and terrible vexations as a minister of Our Lord Jesus Christ.

The exorcist should be aware that there have been, and there are, certain persons who deny that human beings are affected by demonic possession or witchcraft at all, asserting that all such vexations are merely the effects of nature.

They try to demonstrate this in various ways, which we have previously discussed and refuted.

But it is to be noted that when there are signs of a person being possessed by a demon or under the influence of witchcraft, it sometimes happens that similar symptoms could, indeed, be produced by purely natural causes. It is on the basis of such examples that the work of exorcism is sometimes calumniated. The signs of possession and the influence of witchcraft are able to be recognized as real and genuine especially when physicians are unable to provide any explanation, or when all the usual medical treatments for such symptoms have no effects.

We have previously discussed the causes for demonic vexation. In some cases, it is permitted by God because it leads to a greater accumulation of merits. Sometimes it is on account of some venial sin, either of the person concerned or another person. Sometimes it is on account of some mortal sin, either of another person or the possessed person themselves.

There are various signs which are typical of the last variety of cases (i.e. where the demonic possession is the result of a mortal sin of the possessed person). Firstly, when the demon appears to his victim in some hideous and horrible form, either of a human being or a beast of some kind. When these apparitions appear to vanish from the person concerned, they have often, in fact, entered into their body. Such apparitions generally happen at night, or in some obscure and dark place.

The demon can enter through the mouth, ears, or nostrils of the person, in the manner of a wind. Sometimes they send terrible dreams to the afflicted person, causing them to wake up suddenly.

On some occasions when demons enter into a human body, they cause terrible lacerations to appear on the limbs of the person. At other times, the person experiences the sensation of a vessel of extremely cold water being poured down their back, which seems to run from the top of their heads down to the base of their feet.

Although the effect of demons who have taken possession of human beings are virtually innumerable, nevertheless I shall describe some of them so the exorcist may know whether he should proceed with the exorcism, always exercising due caution.

We shall begin with those signs documented in Sacred Scripture. Often demonic possession causes the person to become obstinate and disobedient. This is found in 1 Kings[1] 18, where Saul, who is vexed by a demon, obstinately desires to kill David, for no rational cause.

Sometimes demonic possession turns persons into lunatics, as shown in Matthew 17, where there is a man who says to Our Lord Jesus Christ: "Lord, have mercy on my son, for he is a lunatic." Certain persons are made mute by the demons which possessed them, as shown in Mark 8, where someone says to Christ: "Master, I have taken my son to you, for he has a mute spirit." Again, in Luke 11, Jesus casts out a demon which causes muteness.

There are certain persons who become blind as a result of possession, as is seen in Matthew 12. Hence it is that demons are sometimes called *Lucifuges*, that is, *haters of light*.[2]

Certain demons throw about those they possess, as is clearly seen in Mark 9, where a father of a possessed boy says to Christ: "Whenever the spirit seizes him, it throws him about." Sometimes those who are vexed by demons will grind their teeth, as is shown in the case of the boy just mentioned.[3] Certain demons cause their victim to suffer burns, as is likewise shown in this same case.[4]

---

[1] i.e. 1 Samuel.
[2] Or, more literally, "those who flee the light."
[3] See Mark 9:17.
[4] See Mark 9:21.

Very often demons will cause those they vex to become agitated in the presence of an exorcist. This again is shown in the case of the aforementioned boy, who became very agitated in the presence of the power of the Savior.[5] Sometimes those vexed by demons are thrown down by them and begin to roll around on the ground. This again is exemplified in the case of the boy already cited. They can also cause foam or spittle to come forth from the mouth of their victim, as is likewise shown in the cited case, which says, he was "foaming at the mouth."[6]

Demons can cast the human being they possess into either fire or water, with the intention of killing them. Again, this occurred to the boy in Mark 9.[7] Demons can also cause deafness, as is exemplified in the case of the same boy, for Christ Himself said to the demon: "You deaf and dumb spirit, go out from him!"[8]

It sometimes happens that persons possessed by demons become subject to fury, attacking and inflicting wounds upon those who attempt to exorcize them. This is exemplified in Acts 19, where the case of a demoniac whom certain Jewish exorcists attempt to liberate is described. The possessed man is recounted as rising up and leaping upon the exorcists, leaving them wounded.[9]

There are certain demons that cause the person whom they vex to fall into very grave and incurable illnesses and infirmities. No natural remedy is efficacious against such illnesses and infirmities. This is not surprising, since it is demons hiding within the bodies of their victims which are causing the affliction. An example is the case of the woman who had a "spirit of infirmity" for eighteen years, who was healed by Our Lord Jesus Christ, as is narrated in Luke 13.

---

[5] Mark 9:24.
[6] Mark 9:20.
[7] See Mark 9:22.
[8] Mark 9:25.
[9] See Acts 9:13-16.

There are certain other signs by which a possessed person may be recognized, which are listed in the *Liber Sacerdotalis*.[10] For example, one sign of possession is that a person's eyes begin to take on a frightening or terrible appearance. Still others have their limbs horribly attacked and contorted by demons, which may even cause their death, unless they are promptly helped.

There are persons who, as a result of possession, become foolish and constantly indulge in jokes and pranks. In a few cases, demoniacs begin to speak a language foreign to them, even if they have never learned it, or travelled abroad.[11] Certain of them begin to speak Latin coherently, or to sing musically or display knowledge or skills that they would not otherwise have possessed.

But there are many other possessed persons who are rendered stupid and almost insensate. Some are also afflicted with sudden and inexplicable terrors.

The most reliable and powerful sign of the presence of the devil, however, is that the person becomes vexed and agitated when an exorcism is read to them.

---

[10] The *Liber Sacerdotalis* ('Sacerdotal Book') was a volume containing rituals of various kinds (blessings, prayers, exorcisms, etc.), first published by Alberto da Castello, OP, in 1523. It was widely used as a resource by priests in the 16th century.

[11] Note, however, that this is described as a fairly rare occurrence, in Chapter II of *The Scourge of Demons*.

APPENDIX: THE CUDGEL OF DEMONS

CHAPTER XII: THE SIGNS THAT A PERSON IS AFFECTED BY WITCHCRAFT, AND HOW SUCH PERSONS MAY BE DISTINGUISHED FROM THOSE WHO ARE POSSESSED

THERE IS NO doubt that individuals are able to be affected by works of witchcraft, as experience clearly shows. All spells, whether they are intended to arouse amorous feelings or to cause harm, always involve a pact with a demon, whether this pact is clear and explicit, or secret and implicit. Such pacts in themselves are always made in vain.[1] However this may be, the demon attacks the person on whom the spell has been cast and begins to work. Sometimes this happens through the actual presence of the demon in the person afflicted (as in those who are possessed), while at other times the demon exercises its influence externally, without actually entering the person concerned (as in those who are simply bewitched, without being possessed).

---

[1] This is to say that the imagined pact in itself is not really binding upon the demon, although the demon may appear to act as if it is.

All the devices and articles of witchcraft, whether they are found in the victim's bed or in another place—whether such articles are bones, feathers, hairs, grains, pieces of metal, stones, nails, sulfur, etc.—should be removed and burned in a fire which has been blessed, as we have said in our *Flagellum Daemonum.*[2] All this should be carried out without any trace of superstition.

There are various signs by which a person under the influence of witchcraft may be recognized. These are very many and very diverse; nevertheless, I will state those which are to be found in the *Liber Sacerdotalis.* The first is that a person who is bewitched will tend to have a cedar-like color in their face. Others will have a tendency to constriction or squinting of the eyes, drying of the humors of the body, and (in some cases) all the members of their body will feel constricted, as if they were bound.

The strongest sign that a person is either under the influence of witchcraft, or possessed by a demon, or both, is that they feel a constriction of the heart and stomach.[3] Often they may feel that they have a lump of undigested food beneath their stomach. Others feel as is their heart is being pierced, as if by nails; and yet others feel as is their heart is being corroded within them.

There are others who feel intense pain in their neck or in their kidneys, as if these were being lacerated by dogs. Others feel as if there is a great lump in their throat, which seems to ascend or descend. Yet others feel constriction or binding in their reproductive organs.

---

[2] See Chapter VII of *The Scourge of Demons,* above.

[3] The following signs given in this chapter indicated (as is stated) that a person is either under the influence of witchcraft, or possessed by a demon, or both. Clearly, the presence or absence of other signs which relate specifically to possession (some of which are given in the next chapter) would need to be considered in such cases, to determine whether the person is a victim of witchcraft only, or whether they are possessed, or both. If the person is afflicted by witchcraft only, an exorcism may not be required.

Some persons who are either bewitched and possessed (or both) experience an indisposition of the stomach, so that whatever they are given to eat or to drink they physically reject, vomiting it up. Others feel an extremely cold wind, almost with the intensity of fire, which seems to run through their innards. Others find that their ability to digest food is impeded.

A most powerful sign is that when all the usual medical remedies are employed against some symptom of illness, there is no effect at all (as we have stated in the previous chapter). Another sign is the sensation of a continual pulsation in the neck, which can manifest itself in a tremor.

There are other signs that a person is either possessed by a demon, or both possessed by a demon *and* under the influence of witchcraft. These will be detailed in the following chapter.

Appendix: The Cudgel of Demons

Chapter XIII: Signs Which Appear When a Prayer, Adjuration, or Exorcism Is Performed on a Person Who Is Possessed (or on a Person Who Is Both Possessed and Under the Influence of Witchcraft), and the Ways in Which a Demon Departs from a Body

DEMONS OFTEN strive to show, to the best of their ability, that they have not been conquered by means of specific adjurations and commands made against them. Nevertheless, divine power is able to compel them to reveal their presence in the bodies of possessed persons when commanded to do so. The first sign of the presence of a demon is that when a priest places his hand upon the head of a subject, he [the subject] will sense it to be extremely cold, like ice. To some, it feels like an extremely cold wind has entered through their shoulders and descends to their kidneys. Others feel their head become very heavy. Yet others sense that their skull is being constrained or pierced, as if struck by a sword. Others feel an inflammation of the head, face, or even the whole body, as if a fiery vapor is assailing them. Some possessed persons experience a great fever and headache, which seems to debilitate the entire body.

All of these symptoms last only for a short duration [at the beginning of the exorcism or adjuration], for the adjuration or exorcism takes away the power of the demon as it proceeds. Certain persons feel a constriction of the throat, as if they are being strangled. Others sense their stomach to be churning around, as if infested with worms, ants, or frogs. Others vomit violently, or feel extreme torment in their intestines. Quite a few swell up suddenly and severely. Others feel a constriction or piercing of the heart. Trembling may also occur in the limbs of the body which the demons inhabit, like the quivering of a fish or as if ants were crawling over that part of the body.

When undergoing an exorcism, some possessed persons feel that the demon has fled into the space between their flesh and their skin, and is crawling about there like ants under their skin. Others feel that they are being pierced by nails. Sometimes, the demon seems to rush from the head of the person to their feet, or vice versa, like a sudden wind. And there are many other signs which we have witnessed first-hand, for different demons produce different kinds of indications of their presence.

Certain demons are to be found which begin discoursing on the deep mysteries of Sacred Scripture. Sometimes they do this as if forced by God, but their intention is to distract the mind of the exorcist and other persons present, and to draw them into curiosity. If this happens the exorcist should, as far as he is able, compel the demon to be silent.

The exorcist should command the demon to depart from the body of the possessed person, leaving them healthy, free, and unimpeded, and just as they were when they first entered them. The exorcist should also require the demon to give some clear sign that they have really departed, and to take with it all its wicked companions.

Some demons depart from the bodies of their victim like a flame of fire, whereas other pass out like a very cold gust of wind. There are yet others which go out from them in the form of bees or ants. Some go out through the ears, having left the stomach, the heart, or other parts of the possessed person's body.

Certain demons will leave the body in the form of hairs, which continue to protrude from the person's body until the demon has departed. Others go out in the form of frogs, which crawl about inside their victims until they depart. Some demons depart through the nostrils of their victims, flowing to the ground in the form of blood.

There are also many other modes in which demons leave bodies, which we have witnessed in our own experience.

Slaying Dragons Press Classics

Slaying Dragons Press Classics is a new endeavor though one which has long been a desire of the Slaying Dragons Apostolate. In particular, there has been a desire to bring into print the marvelous and largely forgotten works of the master of morality and the spiritual life, St. Alphonsus Liguori.

With the desire to bring back into print many of his excellent writings, there has also been a felt need to make these writings intelligible to the modern Christian mind, often under-catechized and very much immersed in a materialistic and secular culture. Many Christians, even among the devout, have been deprived of the traditional teachings of the Church in the modern era. Great Christian writers such as St. Alphonsus Liguori are, therefore, greatly needed by the modern Church.

Slaying Dragons Press Classics intends to bring back many of his writings, presenting them in a way that preserves the integrity of the original and also presents some helpful analysis to assist the reader in remembering the key teachings.

This effort of bring back into print lost and marvelous writings of St. Alphonsus Liguori will not, God willing, be limited to this great Doctor of the Church alone. It is the hope that this effort will be able to present many more lost spiritual treasures to the faithful of today.

Slaying Dragons Press

Slaying Dragons Press, founded in 2021, is the fruit of a spiritual work begun in 2016 which sought to find new ways to bring people the joy and beauty of the Catholic Faith. By God's Providence, what began under the name *The Retreat Box* has grown into *The Slaying Dragons Apostolate* and *Slaying Dragons Press.*

This work is a grassroots apostolate which thrives on support and endorsements from those who enjoy these books. As a result, fans of the books and supporters of the mission help increase the reach of *Slaying Dragons Press* by telling friends, family, priests, religious, and Bishops about these books.

Please consider supporting this work in any way that you can. While *Slaying Dragons Press* is *not* a non-profit, financial support is always welcome. Please visit SlayingDragonsPress.com for ways to support this apostolate. If you do not have a copy of the other celebrated books we have published, get one today!

Support this work on **Patreon**
~patreon.com/**theslayingdragonsapostolate**

Subscribe to our website for discounts and news
~SlayingDragonsPress.com/pages/**Subscribe**

Popular Titles
from
Slaying Dragons Press Classics

The Life of St. Alphonsus Liguori, by a Member of the Order of Mercy (1886)

A Christian's Rule of Life (with Darts of Fire), by St. Alphonsus Liguori

Sanctifying Pregnancy: In the Light of the Joyful Mysteries of the Rosary, by Margaret Place (1954)

Novena to the Holy Spirit: Prayers and Meditations in Preparation for Pentecost, by St. Alphonsus Liguori

Popular Titles
from
Slaying Dragons Press

Slaying Dragons: *What Exorcists See & What We Should Know*, by Charles D. Fraune [1]

The Rise of the Occult: *What Exorcists & Former Occultists Want You to Know*, by Charles D. Fraune

The Occult Among Us: *Exorcists and Former Occultists Expose the Nature of This Modern Evil*, by Charles D. Fraune

Slaying Dragons - Prepare for Battle: *Applying the Wisdom of Exorcists to Your Spiritual Warfare*, by Charles D. Fraune
- (a study guide, manual, and companion book to Slaying Dragons)

Swords and Shadows: *Navigating Youth Amidst the Wiles of Satan*, by Charles D. Fraune [2]

Come Away By Yourselves: *A Guide to Prayer for Busy Catholics*, by Charles D. Fraune

---

[1] Also available in Spanish and Portuguese.
[2] Also available in Spanish

Slaying Dragons Press

www.ingramcontent.com/pod-product-compliance
Lightning Source LLC
Chambersburg PA
CBHW021641120626
46545CB00002B/657